Religious Pieces
in
Prose and Verse.

Early English Text Society.
Original Series, *No.* 26.
1867, 1914 (*for* 1913).
Price 5s.

Religious Pieces

in

Prose and Verse.

EDITED FROM ROBERT THORNTON'S MS. (Cir. 1440)

IN THE LINCOLN CATHEDRAL LIBRARY,

BY

GEORGE G. PERRY, M.A.,

PREBENDARY OF LINCOLN AND RECTOR OF WADDINGTON,
EDITOR OF *Morte Arthure.*

[*Re-collated with the MS., enlarged and revised* 1913.]

GREENWOOD PRESS, PUBLISHERS
NEW YORK

OXFORD
UNIVERSITY PRESS

Great Clarendon Street, Oxford OX2 6DP
United Kingdom

Oxford University Press is a department of the University of Oxford.
It furthers the University's objective of excellence in research, scholarship,
and education by publishing worldwide. Oxford is a registered trade mark of
Oxford University Press in the UK and in certain other countries

© The Early English Text Society 1867

The moral rights of the authors have been asserted

Database right Oxford University Press (maker)

First Edition published in 1867

All rights reserved. No part of this publication may be reproduced,
stored in a retrieval system, or transmitted, in any form or by any means,
without the prior permission in writing of Oxford University Press,
or as expressly permitted by law, or under terms agreed with the appropriate
reprographics rights organization. Enquiries concerning reproduction
outside the scope of the above should be sent to the Rights Department,
Oxford University Press, at the address above

You must not circulate this book in any other form
and you must impose this same condition on any acquirer

Published in the United States of America by Oxford University Press
198 Madison Avenue, New York, NY 10016, United States of America

British Library Cataloguing in Publication Data
Data available

Library of Congress Cataloging in Publication Data
Data available

Original Series, 26

ISBN 978-0-85-991813-8

CONTENTS

	PAGE
PREFACE	v
I. DAN JOHN GATTRYNGE'S SERMON	1
II. THE MIRROR OF ST. EDMUND	16
III. THE ABBEY OF THE HOLY GHOST	51
IV. WM. OF NASSINGTON'S POEM ON THE TRINITY, &C. .	63
V. THANKS TO CHRIST	75
VI. A PRAYER TO CHRIST	77
VII. A PRAYER FOR MERCY	78
VIII. FIRST HYMN TO JESUS CHRIST	79
IX. HYMN TO JESUS CHRIST AND THE VIRGIN . .	83
X. A PRAYER TO CHRIST	87
XI. MORAL POEM	88
XII. A PRAYER TO JESUS	91
XIII. A SECOND HYMN TO JESUS	92
XIV. OF SAYNTE IOHN þE EUANGELIST . . .	97
XV. EARTH UPON EARTH	106
XVI. SERVE AND LOVE CHRIST	107
XVII. WHAT THUNDER SIGNIFIES	114
XVIII. LAMENTATION OF A DYING SINNER . . .	115
XIX. CHARM FOR THE TOOTHACHE	119
GLOSSARY	121
INDEX OF NAMES	131

PREFACE.

THE miscellany of Religious Tracts and Poems which follows is edited from the Thornton Manuscript, which has already contributed the Morte Arthure and the Hampole Short Treatises to the publications of the E. E. T. S. It is hoped that it will serve somewhat towards illustrating the religious teaching of the fourteenth and fifteenth centuries, as well as towards exhibiting the peculiarities of the Northern English, in which all the pieces are written.

The first tract is a good and idiomatic specimen of a mediaeval Sermon, and as we find that it was preached in obedience to the command of 'oure Fadire þe byschope,' who had directed all those who under him had cure of souls 'opynly, one ynglysche, apone Sonondayes, to preche and teche þaym þat þay have cure off, the lawe and the care to knawe God Almyghty,' it is also at the same time an evidence of the amount of instruction provided for the people in those days. Some hundred years before this Sermon was written, Bishop Grosseteste had given very similar directions to his clergy, mentioning the very heads which are touched in this Sermon, and bidding them discourse of them to the people every Sunday *in idiomate communi*. Surely these facts, and many others like them which might be produced, go far to prove that the parish priest of the Middle Ages was not such a 'dumb dog' as some would have him to be, and that preaching was not confined to the Friars. Dan Jon Gaytrigg must have been a very sensible instructor for his flock, according to their creed and lights; and the nervous and rhythmical English in which his teaching is conveyed would be hard to equal in modern days. There is another copy of this Sermon in the Library of Trinity College, Cambridge, MSS. B. 10. 12, from which Prof. Skeat kindly made an extract for me. It differs very slightly from the text here printed, but has indications of being a somewhat later transcript. For instance, the old and probably not well-known word '*tray*' of the Thornton MS. is changed in the Cambridge copy into 'thoȝt', and an occasional omission of a Northern form betrays the fact that the copier was not writing his own dialect. Mr. Skeat, whose opinion on this subject is of the utmost weight, writes as follows with regard to the style of the Sermon. 'I have not a doubt that the "Sermon" was originally in *verse*, and to print it as prose, without remark, would be a mistake. It is to be noted that the Trinity MS. is at first written as prose (but there are frequent dots shewing where the lines end), and very soon it is written *as verse*, and so continues down to the end. For instance, look at the following:—

> Þe séxte poynt is . þát we sall trówe
> þat þe foúrtyde dáy . áfter þat he ráse,
> thurgh stréngh of hemsélfe . he stéghed vntil héuen,
> whare oure kýnde is nów . in his blýssed pérson,
> noght ánely éuen . no méte til his aúngels,
> bot héghe corounde kýnge . abouén all aúngels.

It is clear that we have here the regular alliterative verse, *perfect* as regards accent, *imperfect* as regards alliteration; in fact, the very kind of metre into which the old Piers Plowman metre would naturally degenerate. The third line preserves the alliteration altogether, and is a nearly perfect line.' Perhaps even a stronger passage than the one selected by Prof. Skeat might be found at page 11:—

> Eúynly to súffire . þe wéle and þe wáa,
> Wélthe or wándreth . whéthire so betýde . . .
> Stýffely to stánde . agáynes our fáas,
> Whéthir þay be bódyly . or þáy be gástely,
> Swa þat ná fulle fándyng . máke vs to fálle,
> Ne be fálse in our fáythe . agaýnes God Almýghtty.

Here the alliteration is very marked. I confess, however, I do not see my way to bringing the whole of the Sermon into this form. If it were originally written in alliterative verse, it would evidently have been with the object of helping the people to commit it to memory.

Treatise No. II is an old English translation of the Speculum of S. Edmund. This was a very popular treatise in its day, and, we believe, the only surviving work of the famous Edmund Rich, Archbishop of Canterbury—famous for his asceticism—famous as a teacher of Greek at Oxford, and as having had for his pupils Grosseteste, Robert, and Roger Bacon—famous for his sudden elevation to the Primacy—notably famous for the good stand he made in that office for English liberties—famous also for his retirement from his high post; and famous after death for the popular tumult which forced the pope to canonize him. All these points are well brought out in Dr. Hook's Life of the Archbishop. At the Monastery of Pontigny in France, the place of his retirement, where the great spirits of Thomas à Becket and Stephen Langton had before him found rest, he wrote, or at any rate finished, his *Speculum*. It is a composition which breathes a fierce asceticism, and is almost Manichean in its hatred of bodily ease. This would insure its popularity in an age which only comprehended religion as a bitter and unsparing chastiser of the flesh, and hence its early translation into French and English. We subjoin a specimen of the original, with the French and English translations. With regard to the age of the latter, Mr. Morris, on examining a passage sent to him, was of opinion that it might be as early as 1350. Very probably it is a rescript from a still earlier English version in a Southern dialect, but I have not discovered any other English MS. of this Treatise.

FRENCH. From Arundel MS. 288. p. 207.	LATIN. (*Original*.) From Magna Bibl. Vet. Patr. XIII. 355.	ENGLISH. Thornton MS. (as printed).
Uidete uocationem uestram.—Ces mo3 de la postle partenent a nous gen3 de religion. uee3, fet il, a quey uous estes apelle3. e ceo dit il por nous exciter a *perfection*. e por ceo qu*el* homme[1] ke ieo pens de moy, mesmes de nuit e de iour, de une part ay ioye gra*nt*. e dautre part gra*nt* dolur. Ioye por la seynte religion. dolur en confusion p*or* ma feble conu*er*sacion. e ceo nest pas grau*nt* m*er*ueyle. Kar Ieo ay gra*nt* acheson. Kar ci dit Seynt Eusebye en un sermon. uenir a religion est souereyne perfecc*ion*. e nent p*ar*fitement uiure souerayne dampnacion. [1] ? houre.	' Videte vocationem vestram fratres.' Ista verba apostoli pertinent ad homines religiosos. Videte (inquit) ad quid vocati estis. Et hoc dixit Apostolus ad excitandum nos ad perfectionem. Et propter hoc quâcunque horâ cogito de me ipso, die vel nocte, ex unâ parte habeo magnum gaudium, et ex aliâ parte magnum dolorem. Gaudium habeo propter sanctam religionem, dolorem et confusionem propter meam debilem conuersationem. Et illud non est mirum, quia habeo magnam causam. Nam, sicut dicit Sanctus Eusebius in vno sermone, Venire ad Religionem summa perfectio est, sed non perfectè viuere in religione, summa damnatio est.	*Videte vocacionem vestram.' This wordes sayse Saynte Paule in his pystyll, and thay are thus mekill to saye one ynglysche, 'See3e 3oure callynge.' This worde falles till vs folke of religioune: and that sais He till excite vs till perfeccyone. And ther-fore what houre þat I thynke of my-selfe, one nyghte or on day, on a syde hafe I gret joye, and on anoþer syde gret sorowe —joy for þe haly religione, sorowe and confusyon for my febill conuersasione. And þat es na wondire for I hafe gret enchesone. Als þe wyese man saise in his sermon, he sais to com to religione es souerayne perfeccyone, and there - in noghte perfitly to lyffe es souerayne dampnacyone.

Among the promises of future publications made by the E.E.T.S. there is held out to us the hope of some day seeing in print the Life of S. Edmund from the British Museum MS. When it is printed I feel persuaded that it will be found very illustrative of the Speculum, and vice versâ. I believe Dr. Hook does not profess to have consulted this old mediaeval Life of the Archbishop for his biography in the third volume of his Archbishops.

We now come to No. III. The Abbaye of S. Spirit. This treatise, of which there are several MS. copies, has been attributed to various authors. Some would have it the composition of Bishop Alcock, who died 1480, but as it exists in the Vernon MS., which is about a century earlier, this notion is disposed of. In the Lambeth MS. it is given to Richard Rolle de Hampole, but as his paternity is claimed for almost all religious Middle-Age MSS. that have gone astray, we cannot build much on that. The fact of the early Vernon MS. having the Treatise in a Southern dialect is much against the supposition of its being Hampole's. Whether Robert Thornton re-wrote it in his own idiom, or how it got into the form we have here, cannot be discovered; but as the preference here given to the Thornton copy may seem to some to be unfounded, we subjoin a conspectus of a portion of four manuscripts for the purpose of comparison.

I. Vernon MS. (Bodleian.) A. D. 1380.	II. Lambeth MS. 432. fol. 37 B.	III. Trin. Coll. Camb. MS. O. 1. 29.	IV. Thornton MS. (as printed).
Here biginneþ a tretis þat is clept þe Abbey of þe holy gost. þat is conscience of monnes herte schulde ben in þis Abbey most.	Here begynnythe Rechard Hamppulle of the Abbay of the holy goest fulle nessessarye.	þis es þe begynnynge of þe abbay of þe holye goste, þe wilke þat es founded in A place þat es callede conscience, and þerfore, mañ, be-whare!	Of the abbaye of saynte Spirite that es in a place that es callede conscyence.
Mi deore Breþren And Sustren. I seo wel . þat monie wolde ben In Religion . but þei mowe not . for Pouert. or for Age . or for drede of heore kun. or for bond of mariage. And þerfore I make her a Book of Religion of herte . þat is of þe Abbeye	Dere Bretheryne and Sustren, I Se welle ther wold be many in Religeoun, but þay may not, for pouerte, or for Awe, or for drede of kyn, or for bondage, or for mariage; therfor y make here a boke of Religeoun of the hert That is of the Abbey of the holy	My fulle dere and well loued brethire and sisters in god, I see now weel in þies dayes þat many meñ wilde full gladely be in religioun, bot þei may nouȝt, fore pouerte or fore elde, or fore dreed, or elleȝ fore kyndrede or for bonde of mariage. And þerfore I make	A dere brethir and systirs, I see þat many walde be in religyone bot þay may noghte, owthir for pouerte, or for drede of thaire kyne, or for band of maryage, and for-thi I make here a buke of þe religeon of þe herte, þat es of þe abbaye of the Holy

of þe holi gost . þat alle þo þat mouwe not ben In bodi Religion þei mowe ben In gostly. Aһ Jhesu Merci . Where may þis Abbey and þis Religion best ben I . founded. Certes neuere so wel . ne so semely . as in a place . þat is clept Concience. Now be houeþ hit þenne . at þe biginnynge . þat þe place of þe Concience be clanset . þorw wyѣ clansynge. þe holi gost senden a doun twey Maidens ful connynge . þat on is clept . Rihtwisnesse. And þat oþer loue of clannesse . þeose tweyne schul caste from þe concience and from þe herte all manere fulyth of foule þouȝtes and of foule ȝeornynges.

goest, that all tho that may not be in Bodely Religeoun myght be in goestly religeoun. A Ihesu mercy where may the abbay of this religeoun be best y foundid. Certis nowhwhere so wele ne so surely as in a place that is callid Consciens. Now hit behovith, at the bygynnyng that the place of the Conscience be clensyd wislye. The holy goest shalle Fynde two maydennys Fulle cunnyng, the tone is callid Rightwisnesse, And the tother is callid love of clennesse. These two shalle cast out from the conscience, and from the hert, alle maner Filthe of foule thoughtes and foule Desyris.

here now a boke of religione of þe herte, þat es, of þe abbaye of þe holy goste ; þat all þoo þat may nouȝt be in bodily religione, þat þei maye godely be in gostely religioun. ¶ A Ihesu, mersy ! where maye þis abbay and þis religione beste be foundeñ and groundede? ¶ Certeȝ, neuer nowere so well ne so stedefastlye, nor ȝit þerto so semely, as right in a placeȝ¹ þat þei calle conscience. ¶ Now þan behoues it firste at þe begynnynge, þat þe place of þe conscience be so enclosede on ilke syde thorough wies closynge, for þis encheson : ¶ Þe holy goste salle do sende two maydens full conande. ¶ þe tone is callede by clerkes Ryghtwysnes ¶ And þe tother is called lufe of grete (?) clennes. ¶ þies two maydenes sall keste fro þe conscience and fro þe herte all manere of fylthes and foule þoughtes, and of foule ȝernynges.

¹ *sic* in MS.; *read* "place."

Goste, that all tho þat ne may noghte be bodyly in religyone, þat þey may be gostely. A Ihesu mercy! Whare may þis abbaye beste be funded and þis religione ? Now certis nowhare so well als in a place þat es called conscyence ; and who so will be besy to funde þis holy religione, and þat may ilke gud crystyne mane and woman do þat will be besy þerabowte. And at þe begynnynge it es by-houely þat þe place of thi conscience be clensed clene of syne, to þe whilke clensynge the Holy Goste sall sende two maydyns þat ere conande, the one es callede Rightwysnes, and þe toþer es called Luffe of clennes. These two sall cast fro þe conscience and fro þe herte all maner of fylthe of foule thoghtes and desyrs.

It seems probable that II, III, and IV have been re-written from No. I in their different dialects, but at any rate this conspectus remarkably illustrates the well-known fact, that mediaeval copiers never kept close to their original, but altered and improved according to their own views of grammar and dialect, without any of that wholesome dread of omitting an inflection which is the scourge of modern editors. The Lambeth MS. in its latter part differs considerably from the Thornton, and contains several passages which the other has not. In fact it may almost better be described as a *similar* treatise than as identical. The Cambridge MS. shews a tendency to insert amplifications and additions, and would thus seem to be later in style, but Mr. Skeat says that the MS. looks like the fourteenth century. There are doubtless several other copies of the treatise to be found.

The matter of this treatise well illustrates the sort of notion which must always have existed even in the most palmy days of monasticism, viz. that it was just possible to live a religious life outside a convent. But the 'Abbaye of S. Spirit' further shews us the reluctance with which this was admitted, the attempt to clothe even active life with the forms, images, and duties of the cloister, and while admitting the possibility of its successful pursuit of holiness, at the same time putting by its side the far higher and more blessed state of the incarcerated regular.

The Religious Poem of William of Nassyngton is certainly not remarkable for its poetical genius, but in the simple scriptural statements of the quondam York lawyer we recognize with pleasure the mind of a devout layman rising out of distracting superstitions to a repose on the great eternal verities of the faith. The Hymns numbered VIII and IX both contain some simple and touching passages. The Moral Poem, No. XI, is by Richard Rolle de Hampole. Hymn No. XIII is among Dr. Furnivall's selections from the Lambeth MSS. There are differences here, but none, it is thought, will object to have two versions of such a beautiful and touching little poem. We now come to the most singular poem of the collection—Saint John the Evangelist. I have not hitherto heard of any other Manuscript of this, and I think all lovers of early English will not fail to be pleased with it.

Indeed some of the words were quite beyond my power, and must have been left unattempted, but for the kind assistance given me in this, and in many other points, by the Rev. W. W. Skeat.

I am afraid, taking the Miscellany throughout, rather a bitter vein of religionism will be found to permeate it. Christianity seems to be regarded as an institution for vexing and harassing the human race, and everything connected with the body and its belongings is simply evil. Manicheeism indeed, as Dean Milman well points out, poisoned the very life-blood of mediaeval Christianity, and Augustine, while he overthrew it as a system, only confirmed and established it as a sentiment. It is probable that this sour asceticism, which has been remarkably illustrated by several publications of the E. E. T. S., will come out even more strongly, as the Society proceeds to dive deeper into the recesses of old English. But this, at any rate, only makes us admire Chaucer the more.

[The text of this book, as far as p. 18, was collated with the Thornton Manuscript by Dr. Furnivall in 1906, and nine new pieces, Nos. V, VI, VII, X, XII, XVI, XVII, XVIII, XIX, were added to its contents. The Dean and Chapter of Lincoln kindly consented to deposit the Manuscript in the British Museum, where the Keeper of the Manuscripts, Mr. Gilson, was good enough to receive it, and a fresh collation of the whole has now been made. Since then the Rev. Canon C. W. Foster of Timberland has very kindly looked up some readings in the MS., and a new Glossary has been provided by Mr. O. T. Williams. J. M.]

I. DAN JON GAYTRYGE'S SERMON.

[*Thornton MS., Linc. Cath. Libr.*, leaf 213 back.]

Here begynnes a Sermoñ þat Dañ Iohn Gaytryge made, þe whilke teeches how scrifte es to be made, & whare-of, and in scrifte how many thyngeȝ solde be consederide. Et est Petrus 4 sentenciarum discrecione primâ.

Als a grett Doctour schewes in his buke, of all þe¹ creatoures þat Gode made in heueñ and in erthe, in water and in ayere, or in oghte elles, þe Souerayne 8 cause & þe skyll whi He mad þam was His aweñ gud will and His gudnes, Thurgh þe whilke gudnes, alls He es all gude, He walde þat some creatures of þase þat He made ware communers of þat blyse þat euer-mare lastis. 12 And for þat na creatoure myghte come to þat blyse †with- owtteñ knaweyng of Godd, als þat clerkes teches, He made skillwyse creatours Angelle and man, of witt and wysdoñ to knawe God Almyghtyñ, and, thorowe þaire knawynge, lufe 16 Hym and serue Hyñ, and so come to þat blyse þat þay ware made to. This manere of knawynge had oure forme-fadyrs in þe state of Innocence þat þay ware mad Iñ; and so sulde we hafe hade, if þay had noghte synnede. Noghte so mekill als 20 hally saules hase now in heueñ, Bot mekill mare þan mañ hase now in erthe. For oure fourme-fadyrs synned, sayse þe prophete, and we bere þe wykkydnes of þaire mysdedis; For þe knawyng þat þay had of Godd Alt-myghteñ, they had it of 24 Goddes gyfte at þaire begynnynge, with-owtteñ trauayle, or tray, or passinge of tyñ. And all þe knaweyng þat we hafe in þis werlde of Hym, es of heryng, and of lerynge, and of techyng of oþer, of þe law and þe lare þat langes till Haly

God's mercy in Creation.

[† lf. 214.]

Man must have knowledge in order to obtain a share in it.

This must be gained by hearing and learning.

¹ MS. yᵉ. When y stands for þ, þ is printed. F.

I. *Gaytryge's Sermon. The Six Things to be learnt by all.*

Kyrke, þe whilke all creato*urs* þat lufes God Almyghten awe to knawe and to cun, and lede þaire lyfe aftir, and swa come to þat blysse þ*at* neu*er* mare blynnes.

And therefore those who have charge of souls must instruct them.

And for-thi þ*at* mekill folke now in þis werlde ne ere noghte wele ynoghe lerede to knawe God Almyghty, ne lufe Hym ne s*er*ue Hym als þay sulde do, and als þaire dedys oftesythes opynly schewes, in gret perell to þam, to lyfe and to saule; and p*er*awnt*er* þe defaute may be in thaym þat hase þair saules for to kepe, and thaym sulde teche,—als p*re*lates and p*er*sons, vicars and prestes, þat ere halden by dett for to lere þam—

Our father the Bishop has ordered all parish priests to instruct the people in their own tongue.

For-thi our Fadir þe byschope þat God Almyghty saue, þat, als Sayn Paule sayse in his pystill, will þat all men be safe, and knawe God Almyghten, and namely þase vndirlowttes þat till hym langes, hase tretide and Ordeyned for þe comon profett, thorowe þe councell of his clergy, þat ilkane þat vndir hym hase cure of saule, Opynly, one ynglysche, apon son*n*ondayes, p*r*eche and teche þaym þ*at* þay hase cure off, þe lawe and þe lare to knawe God Almyghty, þat principally may

In these six things:
(1) The fourteen points of the Creed,
(2) the Ten Commandments,
(3) the Seven Sacraments,
(4) the Seven Works of Mercy,
(5) the Seven Virtues,
(6) the Seven Deadly Sins.

be schewede in theis sexe thynges—[1] In þe fourtene poyntes þat falles to þe trowthe, [2] In þe ten commandeme*n*tes þat Gode hase gyfen vs, [3] In þe Seuen Sacramentes þat er in Haly Kyrke, [4] In þe Seuen werkes of mercy vntill oure euen crystyn, [5] In þe seuen vertus þat ilke man sall vse, [6] And in þe Seuen dedly Synnes þat ilke man sall refuse. And he byddes and co*m*mandes in all þ*at* he may, þat all þat hase cure or kepynge vndir hym Enioyne þair p*ar*ischennes and þair sugettes þat þay here and lere þise ilke sex thynges, and oftesythes reherse þam till þat þay cun þam, and sythen teche þam þair childir, if þay any haue, whate tym so þay

And Parsons and Vicars are to inquire at Lent whether their Parishioners know them.

are of elde to lere þam. And þat p*er*souns and vycars and all p*a*rische prestis, Enquere delygently of þair sugettes In þe lentyn tym, when þay come to scryfte, wheþ*er* þay knawe and cun þise sex thynges; and if it be funden þat þay cun þam noghte, þat þay Enjoyne þam appon his behalfe, and Of payne of penance, for to cun þam. And for-thi þat nane sall excuse thaym thurghe vnknawlechynge for to cun þam,

I. *Gaytryge's Sermon.* (1) *The* 14 *Articles of the Creed.*

ouꝛ haly Fadir ✝ þe beschope, of his gudnes, hase ordaynede and bedyn̄ þat þay be schewede opynly one ynglysche amanges þe folke. [† lf. 214 back.] They are to be explained to folk in English.

4 Whare-fore, anence þe fyrste of þise sex thynges þat es to knawe, þe articles þat falles to þe trouthe,—als gret clerkes teches and schewes in thaire bukes,—Thare Falles to þe faythe[1] fourtene poyntes; Of þe whilke seuen̄ Falles to Goddes Godd- And first of the fourteen Articles of the Creed. Seven are of the Godhead.

8 hede, and oþer seuen̄ Falles to Cristes manehede. ¶ The firste poynte þat we sall trowe of þe Godhede, Es to trow stedfastely In a trewe Godd, and þat na noþer es for to trowe In. ¶ The toþer es, þat þe heghe Fadir of heuen̄ es stedfaste and sothefaste (1) One true God. (2) Father Almighty.

12 Godd Almyghtyn̄. ¶ The thirde es, þat Ihesu Criste, Goddes Sone of heuen̄, es sothefastly Gode, euen̄ till His Fadiꝛ. ¶ The ferthe es, þat þe Haly Gaste, þat samenly commes of bathe þe Fadir and þe Sonne, es sothefaste Godde, euen̄ to þaym̄ bathe; (3) God the Son. (4) God the Holy Ghost.

16 and þe whethir noghte twa Goddes, þe Fadiꝛ and þe Sonne, ne thre Goddes, þe Fadir and þe Sonne & þe Haly Gaste, Bot thre sere persouns, and noghte bot a Godd. ¶ The fyfte arctecle es, þat þe Trynyte, þe Fadir and · þe Sonne and þe Haly Gaste, (5) Three Persons and one God, Maker of all things.

20 thre persouns and a Godd, es makere of heuen̄ and erthe and of all thynges. ¶ The Sexte artycle es, þat Haly Kirke, oure modire, es hallyly ane thorow-owte þe werlde, that es, comonynge and felawrede of all cristen̄ folke þat comouns to-gediꝛ in þe (6) The Catholic Church, the Communion of Saints.

24 sacramentes, and in oþer haly thynges þat falles till Haly Kyrke, with-owtten̄ þe whilke ne es na saule hele. ¶ The Seuend article þat vs awe to trowe es, vppe-rysynge of flesche, and life with-owtten̄ Ende. For when þe dede hase sundyrde oure (7) The Resurrection of the Body and Life Everlasting.

28 bodyes and oure saules for a certayne tym, als oure kynd askes, vnto when̄ þat God sall deme þe qwykke and þe dede, Thane oure saules sall turne agayne till oure bodyes, and we þase ilke (and nane oþer þan̄ we are nowe), sothefastely sall ryse vp in

32 body and saule, þat neuer mare sall sundire, fra þat tym̄ furthe, bot Samen̄ (if we wele doo whiles we er here) wende with Godd to þat blysse þat euer-mare lastes. And if we euyll do, till Endles payne.

[1] 'faythe' crost thru in the MS.

I. *Gaytryge's Sermon.* (1) *The 14 Articles of the Creed.*

Seven points of Christ's manhood.
(1) Incarnate of the Virgin Mary.

¶ Thir are oþer seueñ poyntes of Cristes Manhede þat are nedfull to trowe, till all þat are crystyñ. ¶ The fyrste es, þat Ihesu Criste, Goddes Sone of heueñ, was sothefastely conceyuede of þe madeñ Marie, and tuke flesche and blude, and become man thurghe þe myghte and þe strenghe of þe Haly Gaste, with-owtteñ any merryng of hir modirhede, with-owtteñ any mynynge of hir maydeñhede.

(2) Both God and man.

¶ The toþer artecle es, þat we sall trowe þat He, Godd' and man bathe in a persoune, was sothefastely of þat blessyde maydeñ, Godd' getyñ of His Fadire be-fore any tyme, and mañ, born of His modir, and broghte furthe in tyme.

(3) Suffered for man.

¶ The thirde poynte þat we sall trowe es, Cristes Passione that He tholede bodyly for synfull mañ-kynde, How He was betraysede with His disciple, and takeñ with þe Iewes, beteñ with scourges, þat na skynñ helde, naylede one þe rude, and corounde with thornes, and many oþer harde paynes, and dyede at þe laste.

(4) Descended into Hell.

¶ The ferthe artecle es, þat whene He was dede, and His body tane douñ, and wondeñ and dolueñ, ȝit þe whills His body lay in þe graue, þe gaste with þe Godhede wente vnto Helle, and heryede it, and tuke owte þase þat ware þare-in, als Adam and Eue and oþer †Forme-fadyrs whilke He in His forluke walde þat ware sauede.

[T ff. 215.]

(5) Rose again the third day.

¶ The fyfte poynte es, þat one þe thirde day after þat He dyede, He rase fra dede to lyfe, Sothefaste Godd' and mañ in body and in saule. For als He dyede in seknes of oure manhede, So He rase thurghe strenghe of His Godhede, and swa dystroyed oure dede thurgh His diynge, and quykkynd vs unto lyfe thurghe His rysesynge.

(6) Ascended into Heaven.

¶ The sexte artecle es, þat we sall trowe þat one þe fourtede day eftyr þat He rase, Thurgh strenghe of Hym-selfe, He steye iu-till Heueñ, whare oure kynde es nowe in His blyssyde personne, noghte anely euynne ne mete till His angells, Bot hey coround kynge abowne all His angells, þat be-fore tym̄ was lesse þan þe kynde of angells.

(7) From thence He shall come to judge the quick and the dead.

¶ The seuend article es, þat righte als He dyede, and eftirwarde rase, and stey in-till heueñ, Righte swa sall He come apoñ þe laste day, Bathe for to deme þe qwykke and þe dede, whare all þe folke þat euer was, or es, or sall be, sall sothefastely be schewede and

sene be-fore Hym̄, and ilke a man̄ answere of his awen̄ dedis, and be saued or dampnede wheþer so he serues; For, als His ryghtwysenes now es mengede with mercy, swa sall it thane be
4 with-owtten̄ mercy.

Secundo.
Decem precepta Dei.
The ten Commandementis.

8 ÞE secund thyng of þe Sex to knawe God Almyghten̄ es, þe ten̄ Commandmentes þat He hase gyffen̄ vs. Of þe whilke ten̄, þe thre þat ere firste, awe us hallyly to halde anence oure Godd'; and þe Seuen̄ þat ere eftyre, anence
12 oure euen̄ cristen̄. ¶ The firste comandement charges vs, and teches vs, þat we leue ne lowte na false goddes. And in þis commandement es forboden̄ vs alkyn̄ mysbyleues and · all mawmetryes, all false enchauntementes, and all soceryes, all
16 false charmes, and all wichecraftes, þat men̄ of myssebyleue traystes appon̄, or hopes any helpe In̄, with-owtten̄ God Almyghten̄. ¶ The toþer commandement byddes vs noghte take in ydillchipe, ne in vayne, þe name of oure Lorde Godd',
20 so þat we trowe noghte in His name bot þat es sothefaste, þat we swere noghte by His name bot it be byhouely, and þat we neuen̄ noghte His name bot wirchipfully. ¶ The thirde commandement es, þat we halde and halowe oure haly day,
24 þe Sonondaye, and all oþer þat falles to þe ȝere, þat er ordeynede to halowe thurgh Haly Kyrke. In þe whilke dayes all folke, bathe lerede and lawede, awe to gyffe þam̄ gudly to Goddes seruyce, to here and say it efter þaire state es, in wirchipe of
28 Godd All-myghty and of His gud halowes, noghte þan̄ for to tente to tary with þe werlde, ne lyffe in lykynge ne luste, þat þe flesche ȝernes, Bot gudly to serue Godd' in clennes of lyfe. ¶ The ferthe commandement byddes' vs doo wyrchipe to Fadire
32 and to modire, noghte † anely to fleschely fadyr and modire, þat getes vs and fosters vs furthe in þe werlde, bot till oure gastely Fadire þat hase heuede of vs, and teches vs to lyffe till hele of

Secondly, of the Ten Commandments.

I. The first Commandment.

The second Commandment.

The third Commandment (4th of the Decalogue).

II. The fourth Commandment (5th of the Decalogue). [† lf. 215 bk.]

I. *Gaytryge's Sermon.* (2) *The Ten Commandments.*

oure saules, and till oure gastely modyr, þat es, Haly Kyrke, to be bouxome þare-to, and saue þe ryghte of it, For it es modir till all þat cristenly lyffes, and alswa till ilke man þat wyrchipfull es, for to do wyrchipe eftere þat it es. ¶ The fyfte comandement byddes vs þat we sla na man, þat es to say, bodyly ne gastely noþer; For als many we sla, in þat at we may, als we sclaundire or bakbyte or falsely deffames, or fandes for to confounde þaym þat noghte serues, or withdrawes lyfelade fra þam þat hase nede, if we be of hauynge for to helpe þam. ¶ The sexte commandment forbeddes us to syn or for to foly fleschely with any woman, owþer sybbe or fremmede, wedde or vnwedde, or any fleschely knawynge or dede haue with any oþer þan þe Sacrament of matremoyne excuseʒ, and þe lawe and þe lare of Haly Kyrke teches. ¶ The seuend' byddis vs þat we sall noghte stele: In whilke es forboden vs robbyng and reuyng, and all wrangwyse takynge or with-haldynge, or hydynge or helelynge of oþer menes gudes, agaynes þaire witt and þaire will þat hase ryghte to þaym. ¶ The aughten commandement byddes vs þat we sall bere no false wytnes agaynes oure euen cristen: In þe whilke es forboden vs all manere of lesynges, False consperacye and false swerynge, whare-thurghe oure euen cristyn may lese þayre catell, Faith, Fauour or Fame, or anything ells, wheþer it be in gastely or in bodyly gudes. ¶ The nyende commandement es, þat we ʒerne noghte oure neghtboure house: In whilke es forboden all wrangwyse couetyse of land or of lythe, or of oghte elles þat may noghte be lyftede ne raysede fra þe grounde, als thynge þat es stedfaste, and may noghte be styrrede. ¶ The tend' commandement an þe laste es, þat we ʒerne noghte þe wyefe of oure neghteboure ne of oure euyn cristen, ne his mayden, ne his knaue, ne his oxe, ne his asse: In þe whilke es forboden vs to ʒerne or to take any thynge þat may be styrride of oþer mens gudes, als robes or reches or oþer catell, þat we hafe na gude titill ne na ryghte to; For what thyng so we take or getes one oþer wyse þan þe lawe and þe lare of Haly Kyrke teches, we may noghte be assoylede of þe trespase bot if we

make assethe, in þat þat we may, to þam̄ þat we harmede with
haldande þaire gude. And in case þat we hafe thurghe false
athes, als in assises or oþer enquestes, wetandly or willfully
gerte oure eueñ cristyñ lesse þaire patremoyne or þaire heritage,
or falsely be dyssessede of lande or of lythe, or false deuorce be
made, or any mañ dampnede, þofe all we do þat we may to þe
party, ȝit may we noghte be assoylede of þe trespas, bot of
oure beschoppe, or of hym þat hase his powere, For swylke caas
es ryuely reseruede till hym̄ selueñ. ¶ Thise teñ commande-
menteȝ þat I hafe now rekkenede er vmbylowkede in twa of
þe gospelle. The tane es, þat we luffe Godd' ouer all thynges;
The toþer † es, þat we lufe oure eueñ cristeñ hallely in oure
herte als we do oure selueñ; For Godd awe vs to lufe hally
with herte, with all oure myghte, with all oure thoghte, with
worde and with dede. Oure euyñ crysteñ, als-swa awe vs to
lufe vn-to þat ilke gude þat we lufe oure-selfe, þat es, þat þay
wele fare in body and in saule, and come to þat ilke blysse þat
we thynke to; and whate-so-euer þat he bee, þat þise twa wele
ȝemes, all þe teñ commandementes forsothe he fulfilles.

These Ten Commandments are included in two of the Gospels— that we love God and our brethren.
[† lf. 216.]

Tertio.

Septem sunt Sacramenta Ecclesie.
The Seuene Sacramentes of Haly Kyrke.

ÞE thirde thynge of þe Sex þat I firste touchide, es þe
Seueñ Sacramentes þat Haly Kirke gyffes, thurghe
prelates and oþer prestes þat hase þe powere. Of
whilke seueñ, the first fyve ilke cristeñ mañ awe
lawefully to take efter his elde es; and twa lyes in þaire will
þat ressayues þaym̄. ¶ The firste sacrament of seueñ es oure
'baptym̄,' þat we take þe firste tym̄ þat we be-com̄ cristyñ. In
whilke, bathe þe firste synñ þat we ere borne with, and alkyñ
oþer synnes, ere wascheñ awaye, þat we ere fylede with are[1] we
take it; and þe trouthe of Haly Kyrke es takeñ þare-iñ, with-
owtteñ whilke na synfull mans saule may be sauede. And till
þis sacrament Falles foure thynges, if it sall ryghtely be tane
als Haly Kirke teches. Ane es, ryghte sayeyng and carpyng

The third thing is the Seven Sacraments.

The first is Baptism.

[1 before]

Four things required to make Baptism valid.

of þe wordes þat hym awe for to say þat gyffes þis sacrament, þat ere þise:—'I Baptise þe in þe name of þe Fadir and þe Sonne and þe Haly Gaste.' Ane oþer es, þat it be done anely in watire, For na noþer licoure es lefulle þare-fore. Þe thirde es, þat he þat gyffes þis sacrement be in witt and in will for to gyffe it. And þe ferthe es, þat he þat takes it be, noþer of lerede nor of lewde, Baptisede be-fore; For if þe preste be in were of hym þat sall take it, whethire he be baptisede or he be noghte, þan sall he say þe wordes one þis wyese, 'If þou be noghte baptisede, I baptise þe in þe name of þe Fadire and þe Sone and þe Haly Gaste.' ¶ The secunde sacrament es 'confermynge,' þat þe byschope gyffes to þam þat ere baptisede, þat gyffes thorowe his powere to þam þat takes it þe grace and þe gyfte of þe Haly Gaste, to make þaym mare stalleworthe þan þay ware be-fore, to stande agaynes þe fende and dedly syn; þat nane hase powere to do bot þe byschope allane, þat hase the state and þe stede of Cristes Appostilles. ¶ The thirde sacrament es callede 'penance,' þat es, sothefaste for-thynkynge þat we hafe of oure syn, with-owtten will or thoghte to turne agayne to it. And þis sacrament must haue thre thynges:—Ane es, sorowe in oure herte þat we hafe synnede. Anoþer es, opyn scrifte of mouthe, how we hafe synnede. The [third es, satisfaccion, þat we maun do for oure syn][1].

¶ Þise thre, with gud will to forsake oure syn, clensez vs and wasches vs of alkyn syn. ¶ The ferthe es, 'þe Sacrament of þe Autyr,' Cristes awen body in lyknes of brede, als hale als He tuke it of þe blysside mayden, the whilke, ilke man and woman þat of elde es, awe for to rescheyue anes in þe ȝere, þat es at say, at þe pasch, als Haly Kyrke vses, when þay ere clensede of syn thurghe penance, O payne of doynge owte of Haly Kyrke, bot if þay forbere it by skillwyse cause, þat awe to be knawen to þam þat sall gyffe it; For he þat tase it worthily, tase his saluacyone; and wha-so takes it vnworthily,

---

[1] Lf. 216 b. A sentence is here wanting through error of the scribe. [For 'satisfaccion' see Wm. of Shoreham's Poems 39/1078, 'Sorwe, schryfte, and edbote.' F.]

J. *Gaytryge's Sermon.* (4) *The Seven Deeds of Mercy.*

tase his dampnacione. ¶ The fyfte sacrament es 'þe laste Enoyn-   *The fifth Sacrament is Extreme Unction.*
tynge wit*h* oyle,' þat es halowede and handelyde of prestes ; þe
whilke sacrament awe anely to be gyffen to þam þat he wate
ere of skillwyse elde, and þat he sese sekyrly in perelle of
dede, in lyghtenes and alegeance of þair*e* sekenes, if Godde
will þat þay turne agayne to þe hele, and als in forgyffnes of
venial synnes, and in lessynge of payne if þay passe heþen.

¶ The Sexte sacrament of Haly Kyrke es 'ordire,' þat gyffes   *The sixth Sacrament is Orders.*
powere to þam þat ryghtwysly tase it, For to se*r*ue in Haly
Kirke eft*er* þair*e* state es, and to þam þat takes þe ordyre of
preste, for to synge messe, and for to mynystre þe Sacramentes
of Haly Kyrke, þat to þam fallys, Eftyr þe state þat þay hafe,
and þair*e* degre askes. ¶ The seuend' Sacrament es 'Matry-   *The seventh Sacrament is Matrimony.*
moyne,' þat es, lawefull festyn*n*ynge be-twyx man and woman
at þair*e* bathere assente, for to lyffe samen wit*h*-owtten any
lowssynge, whills þair*e* lyfe lastes, in remedy of syn and getynge
of grace, if it be tane in gude Entente and clea*n*es of lyfe.

The Ferthe thyng of þe Sex.

These be þe Seuen*e* werkes of Mercy Bodyly.

Þe ferthe thynge of þe Sex to knawe Godd' Almyghty, þat   *The fourth thing is the Seven Works of Mercy.*
vs byhoues fullfill in all þat we maye, ere þe seuen
dedis of mercy vntill oure euen cristen, þat Godd'
sall reherse vs apon þe dredfull day of dome, and wiet
howe we haue done þam here in þis lyfe, als sayne Mathewe   *The 7 bodily Works.*
makes mynde in his gospelle. ¶ Of whilke, þe firste es, to   1.
fede þaym þat er hu*n*ngry. ¶ The toþ*er* es, to gyffe þay*m*   2.
drynke þat er thristy. ¶ The thyrde es, for to clethe þam þat   3.
er clatheles or nakede. ¶ The ferthe es, for to herber þam þat   4.
er houseles. ¶ The fyfte es, for to vesete þam þat lyes in   5.
sekenes. ¶ The Sexte es, for to helpe þam þat lyes or er in   6.
presoun. ¶ The Seuend' es, to bery dede men þat hase myst*er*.   7.
¶ Þise ere the Seuen bodyly dedis of mercy þat ilke man awe
to doo þat es myghtty. ¶ Þar are of mercy alswa Seuen gastely   *The 7 spiritual deeds of Mercy.*
dedis þat vs awe to doo till þam þat hase nede till vs. ¶ Ane   1.
es, to consaile and wysse þam þat are wyll. ¶ Anoþ*er* es, to   2.

3. (†lf. 217.) chasty þam þat wyrkkys ill. ¶ Þe thyrd †es, to solauce thaym
4. þat er sorowefull, and comforthe thaym. ¶ The ferthe es, to
5. pray for thaym þat ere synfull. ¶ Þe fyfte es, to be thole-mode
6. when men mysdose vs. ¶ Þe Sexte es, Gladly to forgyffe when
7. men haues greuede vs. ¶ The seuend, when men askes vs for
[1 MS. here] to lere[1] thaym, if we cun mare þan þay, for to lere thaym.
¶ Þise vn-till oure neghtebours ere full nedfull, and to þam þat
duse thaym wondir medefull; For he sall Mercy þat Mercyfull
es; and man with-owtten Mercy, of Mercy sall mysse.

The 7 Bodily Works in 1 line.
vij. opera misericordie corporalia:,: vnde versus:—
Vestio, cibo, poto, redimo, tego, colligo, condo.

The 7 Spiritual Works in 2 lines.
vij. opera misericordie spiritualia:—
Consule, castiga, solare, remitte, fer, ora,
Instrue, si poteris, sic Christo carus haberis.

The Fifte thyng of þe Sex.

The seuene gastely vertus.

The fifth thing is the Seven Virtues.
Group 1 of 3.
Group 2 of 4.

ÞE fyfte thynge of þe Sex to knawe God Almyghten, are
þe Seuen vertus þat Haly Writte teches. Of whilke
seuen, þe thre first þat are hede thewes, teches vs how
to hafe vs vn-to God Almyghtty; and þe foure teches
vs swa for to lyffe þat it be bathe lykande to Godd' and to man.

I. (1) Faith.
¶ Þe firste vertu es 'trouthe,' wharethurghe we trow anely in
Godd' þat made all thynges, with all þe oþer vertus I touchede
be-fore. And þis es nedfull till all þat cristenly lyffes; For
trouthe es begynnynge of all gude dedis; For noþer es trouthe
worthe with-owtten gud werk, ne na werke with-owtten trouthe

(2) Hope.
may pay Godd' Almyghtty. ¶ Þe toþer gude thewe or vertue
es 'hope,' þat es, a sekyr habydynge of gastely gude, thurghe
Goddes gudnes and oure gude dedis, for to com to þat blysse
þat neuer mare blynnes, Noghte anely in trayste of Goddes
gudnes, ne allanly in trayste of oure gude dedis, Bot in trayste
of thaym bathe when þay are bathe Sammen; For noþer sall
we fall sa ferre in-till whanhope þat we ne sall traiste to hafe

þat blysse if we wele do; Ne we saƚƚ noghte com̃ so ferre in-to
ouerhope for to trayste so mekiƚƚ in Goddes gudnes þat we saƚƚ
hope to haue þat blysse with-owtten̄ gude dedys. ¶ Þe thirde   (3) Charity.
4 vertue or thewe es 'charyte,' þe whylke es a dere lufe þat vs
awe vn-tiƚƚ Godd' Almyghtty als for Hym selfe, and tiƚƚ oure
euencristen̄ for God Almyghttyn̄; For þe tane may noghte
be lufede with-owtten̄ þe toþer, als Sayn Iohn þe gospellere
8 sayes in his pystiƚƚ. 'Þat commandement,' he saise, 'hafe we
of Godd'† þat wha-sa-euer lufes Gode, lufes his euencristyn̄. [†leaf 217 back.]
For he þat lufes noghte his broþer wham̃ he may see, how sulde
he lufe God wham̃ he sese noghte?' ¶ Þe ferthe vertue or   II.
  (4) Justice.
12 thewe es 'ryghtwysenes,' þat es, to ȝelde to aƚƚ men̄ þat we awe
þam̃, For to do to ilke a man̄ þat vs awe to doo, for to wirchipe
tham̃ þat ere worthy, For to helpe þe pure þat er nedy, to do
no gyle ne wrange vn-to na man̄, Bot for to do þat skiƚƚ es
16 vntiƚƚ ilke mane. ¶ Þe fyfte vertue or thewe es 'sleghte or   (5) Prudence.
sleghenes,' þat wysses vs to be-warre with wathes of þe werlde;
For it kennes vs to knawe þe gud and þe iƚƚ, and alswa to
sundire þe tane fra þe toþer, and for to leue þat es euyƚƚ, and
20 take to þe gude, and of twa gud thynges for to chese þe better.
¶ Þe Sexte vertue es 'strenghe or stalworthnes,' noghte anely   (6) Fortitude.
of body, bot of herte and wiƚƚ, euynly to suffire þe wele and þe
waa, welthe or wandreth, whethire so betyde, and þat oure herte
24 be noghte to hye for na wele-fare, ne ouermekill vndire for nane
euyƚƚ fare, Bot styffely for to stande agaynes oure faas, whethir
þay be bodyly or þay be gastely, swa þat na fulle fandynge
make vs to falle ne be false in oure faythe agaynes God Al-
28 myghtty. ¶ Þe Seuend vertue and þe laste es, 'methe or methe-   (7) Temperance.
fulnes,' þat kepes vs fra owterage and haldes vs in euenhede,
lettes fulle lykynge and luste of þe flesche, and ȝemes vs fra
ȝernynges of werldly gudes, and kepes in clennes of body and
32 of saule. For methe es mesure and mett of aƚƚ þat we do, if
we lyffe skillwysly als þe lawe teches.

The sexte thyng and þe laste.

ÞE sexte thynge, and þe laste of þase I firste towchede es, þe Seuen heuede or dedly synnes þat ilke a man and woman awe for to knawe to flee and forhewe, For folkes may noghte flee þam bot þay knawe thaym. ¶ Pride ¶ and Enuye, ¶ Wreth ¶ and Glotonye, ¶ Couetyse ¶ and Slouthe, ¶ and Lecherye. And for-þi er þay callede Seuen heuede Synnes, for þat all oþer commes of thaym; and for-þi er þay callede dedely synnes, for þay gastely slaa ilke manes & womanes saule þat es haunkede in alle or in any of thaym. Whare-fore þe wyese man byddes in his buke 'als fra þe face of þe neddyre, fande to flee syn.' For als þe venym of þe neddire slaas manes body, Swa þe venym of syn slaas manes saule. ¶ The firste of þise Seuen synnes es callede 'Pryde,' þat es, a lykande heghenees of a manes herte, Of offyce or of heghe state, or oþer noblaye þat he ouþer haues of kynde or of grace, or he hopes þat he haues mare þan anothire. And of þis wikkede synn commes some sere spyces:—Boste and † auauntynge and vn-bouxsomnes, despite, and ypocrisy and vnhamlynes, and oþer þat ofte ere sene amanges prowde men. ¶ The secunde dedely synn es hatten 'Enuy,' þat es, a sorowe and a syte of þe wele-fare, and a ioy of þe euyll fare, of oure euencristen: Of whilke synn, many spyces sprenges and spredes. Ane es, hateredyn to speke or here oghte be spoken, þat may sown vn-to gude to þaym þat þay hate. Ane-oþer, false juggynge or dome of þaire dedis, and ay turne vn-to euyll þat es done to gude. Þe thirde es 'bakbyttynge,' to saye be-hynde þam, þat we will noghte avowe ne saye be-fore þam; whare noghte anely he þat spekes þe euyll, bot he þat heres it be spoken, es for to blame; For, ware þare na herere, þare ware na bakbyttere. ¶ Þe thirde dedly synn or heuede syn es 'wrethe,' þat es, a wykkede stirrynge or bollenynge of herte, whare-fore a man wilnes for to wreke hym, or wykkydly to venge hym, appon his euyncristyn. And of þis wykkede syn commes stryvynge and

The sixth thing is the seven Deadly Sins,

Called Head Sins because all others spring from them:

(1) Pride.

[†lf. 218.]

(2) Envy.

(3) Anger.

flytynge, with many false athes and many foule wordes, Sclaundere, for to for-do a man's gude fame, Feghtynge and Felony, and ofte manes-slaughtere, and many ma þat nowe es [na] nede for
4 to be neuenede. ¶ Þe fferthe dedly synn men calles 'glotonye,' (4) Gluttony.
þat es, ane vnskilwyse lykynge or lufe in taste or in takynge
of mete or of drynke. And þise trespas men duse apponne sere In 5 ways.
wyse :—Ane es, ouþer ouer arely or ouer late, or ouer oftesythe, 1.
8 for to ete or drynke bot if nede gere it. Ane oþer es, for to lyffe 2.
ouer delycately. Þe thirde es, for to ete or drynke ouer mekyll. 3.
Þe ferthe es, ouer hastely to ete or to drynke. Þe fifte es, to 4, 5.
compas & caste appon whate wyese we may gette dylicious metis
12 or drynkes to fulfill þe lykynges and þe lustes of þe flesch oþer
þan we may gudly lede oure lyffe with, Secundum¹ versum,

Prepropere, laute, nimis ardenter, studiosè. Versus.

¶ Þe fyfte dedly syn es callede 'Couetyse,' þat es, a wrangwyse (5) Covetousness.
16 wilnynge or ȝernynge to haue any maner of gude vs awe noghte.
And þis es donne pryncypally appon twyn wyese. Ane es, In 2 ways.
wrangwysely to get any thynge þat oure likynge or oure lufe 1.
lyghtes apon, als be Sacrelege or by symony, falsehede or okyr,
20 or oþer gelery, whilke þise worldely men er wounte for to vse
þat castes þaire conaundenes swa vn-to couetyse þat þay ne
rekke wheþer it be with ryghte or with wrange, bot þat þay
may gette þat at þaire herte ȝernes. Anoþer es, wrangwisely 2.
24 to halde þat at es getyn, þat es, when we will noghte do to
Godd Almyghten ne till Haly Kyrke, ne till oure euencristyn, þat vs awe for to do by dett and by lawe, bot anely
haldes þat we hafe for ese of oure selfen, whare noghte anely
28 he þat wrangwysly getes, bot he þat wrangwysely haldes, falles
in þe synn. ¶ Þe sexte dedly synn es 'slewthe or slawenes,' (6) Sloth.
þat es, a hertly angere or anoye till vs of any gastely gud þat
we sall do. †And of þis wikkede synn comes sere spyces:— [† lf. 213 bk.]
32 Ane es, latesommes or lyte to drawe apon lenghte or to lache (1) lateness.

¹ MS. 'Sonde,' the probable miscopying of some contraction. Mr. J. A. Herbert suggests 'Secundum,' as the Latin words (not a verse) which follow mean 'Very hastily, delicately, too eagerly, anxiously,' state 4 of the abovesaid 5 ways to be avoided in eating and drinking.

any gude dedis þat we sall do þat may turne vs till helpe or
(2) dullness. hele of oure saules. Anoþer es, a 'dullnes or heuenes of herte'
þat lettes vs for to lufe oure Lorde God Almyghten, or any
(3) idleness. lykynge to hafe in His seruyse. Þe thirde es, 'ydillchipe,' þat 4
ouer mekyll es hauntede, þat makes lathe to begynn any gude
dedis, and lyghtly dose vs to leue when oghte es begunn, and
þare whare we ere kyndely borne for to swynke, als þe feule es
kyndely brede for to flie, It haldes vs euermare in ese agayne 8
oure kynde, For Idillnes es Enemy to cristen man saule,
stepmodire and stamerynge agaynes gude thewes, and witter-
(7) Lechery, wyssynge and waye till alkyn vices. ¶ Þe Seuend' dedely syn
in
es hatten 'lychery,' þat es, a foule lykynge or luste of þe 12
(1) fornica- flesche. And of þis foule syn comes many sere spyces:—Ane
tion,
es 'Fornycacyone,' a fleschely synn be-twyxe ane anlypy man
and ane anlypy woman: and for-thi þat it [es] agaynes þe
lawe, & þe leue and þe lare þat Haly Kirke haldes, it is dedly 16
(2) adultery, syn to þaym þat it duse. Anoþer es 'Avowtry,' and þat es
spousebreke, wheþer it be bodyly or it be gastely, þat greuosere
(3) incest. and gretter es þan þe toþer. Þe thirde es 'Incest,' þat es, when
a man synnes fleschely with any of his sybb frendes, or any 20
oþer þat es of his affynyte gastely or bodyly, wheþer so it be.
Oþer spyces many sprynges of þis syn þat ouer mekill es
knawen and kende in þis werlde with þaym þat ledes þaire
lyfe als þaire flesche ȝernes. 24

¶ Þise are þe sex thynges þat I hafe spoken off, þat þe
lawe of Haly Kirke lyes maste in; The whilke we er
These things halden to knawe and to cun, if we sall knawe God
must be
known if we Almyghty, and come till His blysse. ¶ And for to gyffe 28
would gain
the bliss of ȝow better wyll for to cun thaym, Oure ffadir þe beschope
heaven.
grauntes of his grace Fourty dayes of pardoun till all
þat cunnes thaym, and ratyfyes alswa þat oþer men gyffes,
Swa mekill coueites he þe hele of ȝour saules. For ȝife ȝe 32
conandely knawe þise Sex thynges, thurgh thaym sall ȝe cun
knawe Godd' Almyghty, whaym, als Sayne Iohn sayse in his
gospelle, cunnandely for to knawe swylke als He es, It es endles
lyfe and lastande blysse. To þe whilke blysse He brynge vs, 36

oure Lorde Gode Almyghty! Ameñ! Ameñ! Ameñ! *Per Dominum nostrum Iesum Christum, qui cum* Deo patrê[1] et Spiritu Sancto viuit *et* regnat *omnipotens* deus in *secula seculorum.* Amen! Amen! Amen!

[1] MS. patri.

[The 'Hymn to Jesus Christ'—Ihesu, thi swetnes, wha moghte it se— printed on pages 92-6 below, follows here in the MS., on leaf 219.]

II. THE MIRROR OF SAINT EDMUND.

[*Robert Thornton's MS., Lincoln Cathedral Library*, lf. 197.]

¶ Incipit Speculum Sancti Edmundi Cantuar*ensis* Archipiscopi in Anglicis[1].

Here begynnys The Myrro*ur* of Seynt Edmonde þe Ersebechope of Cant*er*berye.

I[2].

The writer addresses himself to the folk of religion, and exhorts them to live perfectly.

*V*IDETE *vocacionem vestram.* This wordes, sayse Saynte Paule in his pistyll, and thay are thus mekill to saye one ynglysche, 'Seese ȝowre callynge.' This worde falles till vs folke of religiou*n*: and þat sais he, till excite vs till p*er*feccyone. And ther-fore, what houre þat I thynke of my-selfe, one nyghte or on day, On a syde hafe I gret Ioye, and on anoþ*er* syde gret sorowe :—Ioy, for þe haly religio*n*; sorowe and co*n*fusyo*n* for my febill con*uer*sasione. And þat es na wondire, for I hafe gret encheso*n*. Als þe wyese man saise in his s*er*mo*n*, he sais, 'to com to Religio*n* es sou*er*ayne p*er*feccyone; and there-in noghte p*er*fitly to lyffe, es sou*er*ayne dampnacyone.' And thar-for þare es na turne of þe way bot ane, to come in congregacyone, þat es, to drawe to p*er*feccione als þou will þi saluacyone, to leue all þat es in this worlde and all þat þer-to langys, and sett thi myghte to lyffe p*er*fitly. To

II.

Perfect living consists in living honourably, meekly, and lovingly. 'Honourably' implies doing God's will in all things.

lyffe p*er*fitly, as Sayne Bernarde vs kennys, þat es, to lyffe honourabilly, mekely, & lufesomly. Hono*ur*abilly, als to God, þat þou sett thy*n* Entente to do Hys will, þat es [at] say in all thynges þat þou sall thynke in hert, or say w*ith* mouthe, or doo in dede, w*ith* any of þi fyve wittes; alls w*ith* seynge of eghe,

4

8

12

16

20

24

---

[1] *Verbis* understood.

[2] The numbers I, II, &c., at the side are not in the MS., but are appended to mark the chapters of the original Latin work.

II. St. Edmund's Mirror. Need of Knowing Ourselves.

Herynge of Ere, Smellynge of neese, Suellynge of throtte, towchynge of hande, Gangand, or standande, Lygand, or sittande, thynke at þe begynnynge if þat it be Goddes wiłł or noghte. 4 And if it be Goddis wiłł, do it at thy powere. And if it be noghte Hys wiłł, do it noghte, for to suffre þe dede.

Bot now may þou aske mee 'what es Goddes wyłł?' I say þe, His wiłł es na noþer thynge bot þi halynes. Als þe Appostiłł in 8 his pystiłł :— ¶ **Hec est Voluntas Dei, Sanctificacio vestra :** Þat es to say, þat es Goddes wiłł, þat 3e be haly. Bot now may þou aske me: 'What mase man haly?' I say þe, twa thynges with-owtten ma, þat es, knaweynge and lufe. Knaweyng of 12 sothefastnes, and Lufe of gudnes. Bot to þe knaweynge of Godde, þat es sothefastnes, ne may þou noghte com̄ Bot be knaweynge of thi selfe; ne 3it to þe luf of Godde may þou noghte com̄, bot thurghe þe luf of thynn̄ evyn̄-crystyn̄. 16 To þe knaweyng of þi selfe may þou com̄ with besy vmby-thynkynge; And to þe knaweynge of Godde thurghe pure contemplacionne. To þe knaweynge of þi selfe þou may com̄ on̄ þis manere: Thynke besely and ofte what þou erte, 20 what þou was, and what þou sałł be. Fyrste, als vn-to þi body: þou erte now vylere þan̄ any mukke; þou was getyn̄ of sa vile matire and sa gret fylthe, þat it es schame for to nevynn̄, and abhomynacyon̄ for to thynke; þou sałł be 24 delyuerde to tades and to neddyrs for to ete. What þou has bene and what thow erte, now sałł þou als to þi saule, thynke, For what þou † sałł be þou may noghte wyete nowe. Vmbe-thynke þe nowe how þou has don̄ gret synn̄s and many, 28 and how thou has lefte gret gudnes and many. Thynke how lange þou hase lyffede, and what thow has rescheyuede, and how þou has dyspende it. For ilke an houre þat þou has noghte thoghte one Godde, þou has it tynte. For þou sałł 32 3elde resonne of ilke-ane ydiłł thoghte, of ilke-ane ydiłł dede, of ilke-ane ydiłł worde. And righte as þou has noghte ane hare of thi heuede þat it ne sałł be gloryfyede, if swa be þou be safede, Righte swa sałł eschape nane houre þat it ne sałł [be] 36 accountede. A Ihesu, mercy! If ałł þis worlde ware fułł of

Marginal notes:
What the will of God is, viz. that we should be holy.

III.

Holiness consists in knowing and loving.

To know God we must know ourselves.

Reflect then on thyself. Thou art made of vile corrupting matter.

[† leaf 197 bk. Thow *rep.*]
Thou hast done many sins.
[MS. Thou sall.]

Thou must give account of all.

smalle powdire, wha sulde be sa qwaynte þat he sulde or moghte
Iugge ilke a thoghte, ilke a sawe, ilke a dede by þam̄ selfe,
and twyn̄ ilke ane fra oþer? Certis na thynge bot þe saule,
þat es a thowsande sythes gretter þan all þis worlde, if it ware 4
a thowsande sythes gretter þan it es. And it es so full of
dyuerse thoghtes, lykynges and ȝernynges, wha moghte þan
thus seke his herte þat he moght knawe all þat es þare-in
or thynke it? See nowe, my dere hertly frende, howe þou 8
has gret nede of knawynge of thi selfe. Sythen̄ aftyrwarde
take gude hede whate þou erte nowe, als vn-to þi saule; howe
þow has littyll of gude in the, and littill of witte and littill
of powere; For þou ȝernys ilke a daye þat at noghte avayles 12
the, and euer mare ouer lattly þat at may availe the. Dere
frende, þou erte dessayfede sa ofte with vayne Ioye; nowe
trauelde with drede, nowe erte þou lyftede one lofte with false
trayste. See now on þe toþer syde:—Þou ert chaungeabill: 16
þat at þou will doo to day, þou will noghte to morne. And
ofte sythes þou erte anoyede eftire many thynges, and turment
if þou hafe thaym noghte. And sythen when þou has þam at
þi will, þan erte þou of thaa thynges annoyede. Thynke ȝitt 20
one þe toþer syde, how þou erte lyghte to fande, frele to agaynestande, and redy to assente. Off all þese wrechidnes now has
þe delyuerde Ihesu þi spouse, and delyuers þe ylke day mare
and mare. For when̄ þou was noghte, He mad þe in saule 24
aftire His awen̄ lyknesse and His ymage, and þi body made
of foule stynkande skyūm of þe erthe, whare-of es abhomy-
nacyone to thynke, He mad þe in witte and in membirs sa nobill
and sa faire þat nane can̄ deuyse. Thynke now besyly, ȝe þat 28
has fleschely frendis and kynredyn̄, why ȝe luffe þam̄ sa derely
and sa tendirly. If þou say þat þou lufes þi fadire or þi modire
for-thi þat þou ert of þaire blude and of flesche getyn̄, Sa are
þe wormes þat comes of þam̄ day be day. On a-noþer syde 32
þou has noþer of þam̄ body ne saule, Bot þou þan has of God
thurghe thaym̄. For whate sulde þou hafe bene if þou had
duellyde swilke as þou was of thaym̄, when þou genderide
in fylthe and in syn̄? One þe toþer syd, if þou lufe brethire or 36

Marginal notes: It is hard to search out all that is in the heart of man. — Our shortcomings and imperfections are manifold. — Jesus the only deliverer from weakness and wretchedness. — He ought to be loved more than earthly friends.

II. St. Edmund's Mirror. The Infinite Mercy of Jesus.

systers or oþer kynredyn, for-thi þat þay are of þe same flesche of fadir or of modire, and of þaire blude, by þe same skyll solde þou lufe a pece of þaire flesche if it [ware] schorne a-waye; and
4 þat solde be errour gret with-owtten mesure. ȝyfe þou say þat þou lufes þam for-thi þat þay hafe fleschely fegure in lyknes of man, and for-thy þat þay † haue saule ryghte als þou has, þan es þi broþer fleschely na nerre þan anoþer; bot in als mekill als
8 þou and he hase bathe a fadire and a modire fleschely, The begynnynge of þi flesche, þat es, a lyttill filth, stynkande and full to see. Thare-fore þou sall lufe Hym of whaym all þi fairenes commes. And þou sall lufe gastely ilk a man, and
12 flee fra now-forthwarde to lufe fleschly.

Reasons why we should love Jesus.

[† leaf 198.]

IV.

And swa sall þou doo certaynly if þou conabilly thynke of gudes þat He has done gudly for þe; and mare sall doo if þou lufe Hym enterely; For, als I saide at þe begynnynge,—when
16 þou was noghte, He made þe of noghte; and when þou was tynte, He fande þe; and when þou was peryschede, He soghte þe; and when þou was saulde with syn, þan He boghte þe; and when þou was dampnede, þan He sauede þe. And when
20 þou was borne in syn, He baptyȝede þe; and sythen aftirwarde, when þou synnede sa foully and sa ofte, þan He sufferde þe so frely, and habade thynne amendemente sa lange, and sythen rescheyuede þe sa swetly, and þe has sett in sa swete a falachipe.
24 And ilke a day when þou mysdose, þan He reprofes þe; and when þou repentis þe, þan He forgyffes the; and when þou erris, þan He amendis þe; and when þou dredis þe, þan He leris þe; and when þou hungers, þan He fedis þe; and when
28 þou erte calde, þan He warmes þe; and when þou has hete, þan He kelis þe; and when þou slepis, þan He saues þe; and when þou rysez vpe, þan He vphaldes þe; and euer-mare when þou erte at male eese, þan He comforthes þe. Thyre gudnes, and
32 many oþer, hase done vnto þe thi swete spouse Ihesu Criste. And þe swettnes of His herte sall þou thynke euer-mare, and euer speke þare-of, and euer-mare lofe Hym, and euer thanke Hym, and that bathe nyghte & day, if þou oghte kan of lufe.
36 And þare-for, when þou ryses of þi bedde at morne or at

The infinite mercies of Jesus.

He always forgives us when we repent.

The service that we owe to Him.

V.

mydnyghte, thynke als tite how many thowsand men & women ere perischede in body or in saule þat nyghte: Some in fyre, Some in oþer manere, als in water or one lande; Some robbide, woundide, Slayne, dede sodanly with-owttyn sacramentis, and fallyn in-till dampnacione ay lastande. Thynk alswa how many thowsande þat nyghte are in perill of saule, þat es to say, in dedly syn, als in glotony, lechery, Couetyse, in manes-slaynge, and in many oþer folyes. And of all þise illes, the has delyuered thy swete Lorde Ihesu, with-owtten þi deserte. What seruyce hase þou donne, whare-fore He hase þusgate keped þe, and many oþer loste and forsaken? For sothe, if þou take gud kepe how gret gude He has done þe on ilk a syde, þou sall fynd hym ocupiede aboute þi profet, als He did nan oþer thynge, bot anely ware entendande to þe and to þi hele, als if He had forgetyn all þis worlde for to be anely intendand vn-to þe. ¶ And when þou hase þis thoghte, lyfte vpe thi handis and thanke thi Lorde of þis and of all †oþer gudes, and say one þis manere, 'My[1] Lorde Ihesu Criste! grace I ȝelde; and thanke þe, þat me, thyne vnworthy seruande, þou hase kepid couerde and vesete in þis nyghte (Or in þis day), hale, safe, and wemles vn-to þis tym þou hase made to come, and for all oþer gudes and benefitis þat þou hase geffyn me, anely thurghe þi gudnes and þi pete, þou þat lyffes and regnes endles. Amen.' Dere frende, in þis same manere sall þou say when þou rysez at morne, and when þou lygges down at evyn. And when þou has done swa, þan sall þou besyly thynke how þou hase spende þat day (or þat nyghte), and pray God of mercy of þe ill þat þou hase done, and of þe gude þat þou hase lefte vn-till þat tym. And, dere frende, do na thynge in þis lyfe till þou commend þi selfe, and thi frendes qwykke and dede, in the handis of thi swete Lorde Ihesu Criste, and say one þis maner, 'Lorde[2] Ihesu Criste! in

[† leaf 198 bk.]
The prayers we ought to offer to Christ.

Do nothing till you've commended yourself and your friends to God by prayer.

---

[1],[2] These prayers are first given in the MS. in Latin—*Gracias tibi* . . . *In manus tuas* . . .—the translation immediately following. It did not seem necessary to print the Latin as well, the English being a full equivalent. The translation in the first case is introduced with the words 'This Oryson es þus to say one Inglysche my Lorde,' &c.; and in the second 'And þis orysone es þus mekill to saye Lorde' &c.

II. St. Edmund's Mirror. Contemplation of God.

þi handis, and in þe handis of thyn haly Angells, I gyffe in *The Prayer to Jesus Christ.*
þis nyghte (or in þis day) my saule and my body, my Fadir
and my Modire, my brothire and my systirs, frendis and
4 seruandes, neghtburs and kynredyn, my gude-doers, and all
folke righte trowande. Kepe vs, Lorde, in þis nyghte (or
þis day) thurgh þe gud dedis and þe prayere of þe blyssed
mayden Marie and all thi halous, fra vices and fra wykked
8 ȝernyngez, fra synns and fra fandynges of þe deuell, fra sodayne
and avysede dede, and fra þe paynes of helle. Lyght my
herte of the Haly Gaste and of thi haly grace! Lorde! þou
make me to be bouxsome euer-mare to þi byddynges, and suffire
12 me neuer mare to twyn fra the, endles Ihesu, Lorde in Trinite!
Amen!' My dere frende, if þou hase þis manere, þan sall þou *Thus we may obtain the knowledge of ourselves.*
hafe verray knaweynge of thi selfe, For thus saise haly Writte,
'If þou †trayste one thy selfe, to þi selfe þou sall be takyn; [†leaf 199.]
16 and ȝif þou trayste one Gode and noghte one þi-selfe, to God
þou sall be gyffen.' And þis maner of consederatyone es
callede 'medytacyone,' For by þis maner of knawynge of þi
selfe, & by þis maner of medytacyone, sall þou come to þe
20 knaweynge of Gode, by haly contemplacyone.

Wiet þou þat þare es thre manere of contemplacyone. The VI.
fyrste es in creaturs. The toþer es in haly scripture. The *The three different sorts of contemplation:*
thirde es in Gode hym-selfe in His nature. Thow sall wyet þat
24 contemplacyone es na noþer thynge bot thoghte of Godde
in gret lykynge in saule, And to se His gudnes in His creaturs.
His gudnes in His creaturs may þou see one þis manere. Thre *Contemplation of the works of God;*
thynges pryncypaly ere in Gode, þat es to say, Myghte,
28 Wysdome, and gudnes. Myghte es appropirde to Godd þe
Fadire. Wysdome, to God þe Son. Gudnes, to God þe Haly
Gaste. Thurgh Goddes myghte ere all thynges made, and
thurgh His wysdome ere all thynges meruailously ordaynede;
32 and thurgh His gudnes ilke a day ere all thynges waxande.
His powere may þou see by þaire gretnes and by thaire makynge;
His wysdom by þaire fairenes of þaire ordaynynge; His gudnes
may þou see by þaire Encressynge. Þaire gretnes may þou see
36 by þaire four partynges, þat es to saye, by þaire heghte, and by

þaire depnes, and by þaire largenes, and by þaire lenghe.
His wysdom may þou see if þou take kepe how He hase gyffen
to ylke a creature to be. Some He hase gyffen to be anely,
with-owtten mare, als vn-to stanes. Till oþer to be & to lyffe, 4
als to grysse and trees. Till oþer to be, to lyffe, to fele, als
to bestes. Till oþer to be, to lyffe, to fele, and with resone
to deme, als to mane and to angells. For stanes erre, bot
þay ne hafe nogte lyffe, ne felys noghte, ne demes noghte. 8
Trees are; þay lyffe, Bot thay fele noghte. Men are; þay
lyffe, þay fele, and þay deme, and þay erre with stanes, [þay] lyffe
The excellence of man's nature; with trees, þay fele with bestes, and demys with angells. Here
sall þou thynke besyly þe worthynes of manes kynde, how it 12
ouer-passes ilke a creature. And þare-fore saise Saynt Austyn,
'I wald noghte hafe þe stede of ane angelle, if I myghte hafe
þe stede þat es purvayede to man.' Thynk also þat man es
worthy gret schenchipe þat will noghte lyffe eftyre hys degre 16
and eftyre his condicyone askis; For all þe creaturs in þe
All creatures made for him. worlde ere made anely for man. Þase þat ere meke, ere made
for thre skylles; For to helpe vs at trauayle, als nate, Oxen,
kye and horse; For to couer vs & clethe vs, als lyne, and wolle 20
and lethire; for to fede vs and vphalde vs, als bestes, Corne of
þe erthe, Fysche of þe See; and þe noyande creaturs, als ill trees
and venemous bestes, þe wylke are made for thre thynges, For
oure chastyyng, for oure amendement, and for oure kennynge. 24
We ere chastied and puneschet, when we ere hurte. And þat
es gret mercy of Godde, þat He will chasty vs bodyly þat we be
[† leaf 19) bk.] noghte puneschet lastandly. † We erre amendid when we
thynke þat all þese ere broghte vs for oure syn. For when 28
we see þat sa lyttill creaturs may noye vs, þan we thynke
one oure wrechidnes, and þan we ere mekyde. We ere Eftirwarde kende, for-þi þat we see in þise creaturs þe wondirfull
werkes of God oure Makere. For mare vs availes till oure 32
ensampill and Edifycacione, þe werkes of þe pyssmowre þan
dose þe strenghe of þe lyone or of þe bere. Als-swa, righte
als I haue said of bestes, reght swa vndirstande of trees; and
when þou hase donne on þis manere, Raise vp thy herte vn-till 36

Godd͞, and thynke how it es grete myghte to make aⅱ thynges of noghte, and to gyffe þam to bee, and grete wysdom͞ to ordayne þam in sa gret fairenes, and in swa gret bounte, to multyply
4 þam͞ ilk a day for oure prowe. A! mercy Godd͞! how we are vnkynde! We dyspende aⅱ His creaturs, and He þam makes ! *The thoughts this should*
We co*n*found þam͞, and He þam gou*er*nes. We distruy þam͞ *cause in us.*
ilke a day, and He þam multyplies. And þare-fore say tiⅱ
8 Hym in thi herte, 'Lorde! for-þi þat þou arte, þay ere, and for-þi þat þou arte fayre, þay are faire; and for-þi þat þou arte gude, þay are gude. W*ith* gud ryghte þay loue þe, and Onoures þe, and gloryfyes þe, aⅱ thy creatur*es*. O blyssed Godd in
12 Trinyte! w*ith* gud ryghte þay loue þe for þaire gudnes, w*ith* gud ryghte þay anoure*n* þe for thaire fairenes, with gud righte þay glorifye þe for þaire profet, aⅱ þi creaturs, blyssed Trinyte! Of wham͞ aⅱ thynges ere thurgh His powere made; Thu[r]gh
16 whaym aⅱ thynges are thurgh Hys wysdom͞ gou*er*nede; In whaym aⅱ thynges are thurgh His bounte multipliede; Tiⅱ Hym hono*ur* and louynge w*ith*-owte*n* [ende]. Ame*n*!'

20 ÞE toþ*er* degre of contemplacyone es in Haly Wryte. *ij*ᵃ *pars.*
Bot nowe may þou say to me, 'I þat knawes na letters, VII.
how may I eu*er* mare com to co*n*templacyone of Haly *The second sort of con-*
Writte?' Now, my dere frende, vndirstande me swetely, and *templation is of Holy*
I saⅱ say p*er*chance to þe aⅱ þat es wrete*n*, if þou ka*n* noghte *Writ.*
24 vndirstand Haly Writt. Here gladly þe gud þat me*n* saise þe: *How the*
and whe*n* þou heres Haly Wryte, owþer in s*er*mo*n* or in p*r*iue *unlearned may profit by*
collacyone, take kepe als tyte, if þou here oghte þat may availe *Holy Writ.*
þe tiⅱ edyfycacyo*n*, to hate sy*n* and to lufe vertue, and to
28 dowte payne, and to ȝerne Ioye, To dispyse þis worlde, and to hye to blysse, and whate þou saⅱ doo and whate þou saⅱ lefe, and aⅱ þat lyghtes þi*n*ne vndirstandynge in knawynge of sothefastnes, and aⅱ þat kyndiⅱs þi lykynge in brynnynge
32 of charite; For of þise twa gudnes, es aⅱ þat es wrety*n* in preue or in apperte. Owte of haly writte sall þou drawe and cu*n* witte, whilke are þe seue*n* dedly synnes, and þe seue*n* vertus, and þe ten †comandmentis, and þe tuelfe artycles of [†leaf 200.]
36 þe trouthe, and þe seue*n* sacramentis of Haly Kyrke and þe

seuen gyftis of þe Haly Gaste, and þe seuen werkes of mercy, and þe seuen vertuz of þe Gospell, and þe seuen prayers of þe pater noster.

VIII. Þir are þe seuen dedly synnes :—

The seven deadly sins.
(1) Pride. Its seven disobeyings to God.
Pryde and Envy, Ire, Slouth, Couetyse, Glotony and Lechery. Pryde es lufe of vnkyndly heghyng; and þar-of comes þir seuen vnbouxomnes agayne God, or agayne souerayngne, þat es to say, to lefe þat þat es commandyd, and to do þat that es defendyde. The toþer branch of pride es

(2) Surquedry.
surquytry, þat es, to vndirtake þyng ouer his powere, or wenys to be mare wyse þan he es, or better þan he es, and auauntez hym of gude þat he hase of oþer, or of ill þat he hase

(3) Hypocrisy.
of hym-selfe. The thrid braunche of pride es ypocrisye, þat es, when he feynys hym to hafe gudnes þat he hase noghte,

(4) Contempt.
and hydes þe wykkednes þat he hase. The ferth braunch of pride es despyte of thyne euencristen, þat es, when man lesses

(5) Excuses.
gudnes of oþer, for-thi þat hym selfe suld seme þe bettir. The fyfte braunche, þat es, when man makes lyknes be-twyx his awen wykkednes and oþer mens wikkednes, þat his awen may

(6) Shamelessness.
seme þe lesse. The sexte braunche of Pryde es vnschamefulnes,

(7) Elation.
þat es, when men hase noghte schame of ill ded aperte. The seuen braunche of pryde es Elacion, þat es, when a man hase heghe herte, þat he will noȝte suffire to felawe ne mayster.

Man prides himself on three things.
Dere frende, þou sall wit þat thre þynges ere, whare-of a man Enprides hym, þat es to say, of þe gudez þat he hase of kynde,

1. als fairenes or strenghe or of gude witte or of nobille kynredyn.
2. The toþer þyng es þat men hase of purchase, als cunnynge,
3. Grace, gud loos, or dygnyte or offyce. The thirde þynge es erthely þynge or erthely gude, als clethynge, houssynge, Rentez, Possession, Menȝe, horssyng, and honour of þis worlde. Pride makes man to be of gret herte and heghe, to despyse his euencristen, and to ȝerne heghenes and maystry ouer oþer.

(2) Envy.
The toþer dedly syn es 'Envy.' And þat es, Ioye of oþer mens harme, and sorowe of oþer mens wele-fare. And þat may be in herte with lykynge, or in mouth with bakbyttynge, or in werke with of mens gudnes wythdrawyng, or ells with ill procurynge.

Envye mase man to hafe þe herte hevy of þat he sese oþer men
mare worthi þan he in any thyng. The third dedly syñ es (3) Anger.
'wretħe,' þat es, ane vnresonabyłł temperoure of herte; and of it
4 comes stryfes and contekes schamefułł, and dyuerse wordes, and
deuyouse and wikked sclandirs. † The fertħe dedly syñ es (4) Sloth.
'slouthe;' and þat mase manes herte hevy and slawe in gude [† leaf 200 bk.]
dede, and makes mañ to yrke in prayere or halynes, and puttes
8 man in wykkednes of wanhope, for it slokyns þe lykynge of
gastely lufe. ¶ The fyfte dedly syñ es ' couetyse,' and þat es, ane (5) Covetous-ness.
vn-mesurabiłł luffe to hafe erthely gudes; and it destroyes &
blyndes manes herte. And þare-of commes tresones, False
12 athes, wykked reste, Malice, and hardnes of herte agaynes
mercy. ¶ The sexte dedly syñ es 'glotony;' and þat makes mañ (6) Gluttony.
to serue and to be bouxome tiłł wykked lykynges of þe flesche,
þe whilke man suld maister and ouercome with mesure. Of
16 glotony commes vayne Ioy, lyghtnes, and littiłł vndirstandynge.
¶ The seueñ dedly syñ es ' lecherye;' and þat mase manes herte (7) Lechery.
to melte, and to playe thare þare his herte lykes, and heldes,
and þat with-owteñ gouernynge of resoune. Of lechery
20 commes blyndynge of herte, in prayere vnstabilnes and fulle
hastynes, lufe of hym selfe, hatredeñ of Godde, lufe of þis
worlde, vgglynes, and whanhope of þe blysse of heueñ. ¶ Dere Why these are deadly
frende, thire are þe seueñ dedly synnes; and wele ere þay callid sins.
24 dedly synnes, For Pride twynnes fra man his Godde, Envy his
euencristeñ, Ire hym-selfe twynnes, Slouthe hym tourmentes,
Couetyse hym be-gyles, Glotony hym dessayues, and Lecherye
hym in thraledome settis.
28 Nowe hase þou herde þe seueñ sekenes of manes saule. IX.
¶ Sytheñ aftirwarde commes þe souerayne leche, and takes þere
medcynes, and waresche mañ of þese seueñ seknes, and stabiłłs
hym in þe seueñ vertus3, thurgh þe gyftes of þe Haly Gaste.
32 Þe whilke are þese, ¶ þe gaste of wysdom and vndirstandynge, The seven Christian
þe gaste of consaile and of stalworthenes, þe gaste of cunnynge Virtues.
and of pete, and þe gaste of drede of Godde Almyghty. Thurghe
þese gyftes oure Lord Ihesu lerres mañ ałł þat he hase myster
36 tiłł þe lyfe þat es callid actyfe, and til þe lyfe called contem-

platyfe. And se howe firste, man suld lefe þe euyll and do þe
gude: lefe þe euyll, þat teches vs þe gaste of drede of Godd'
Almyghty; and do þe gude, [þat] leres vs þe gaste of pete.
And for-þi þat twa thynges are þat lettis vs to do gude, that
es at saye, wele-fare and tribulacione of þis worlde; For wele-fare
desayues vs with losengery, tribulacion with hardnes of noyes
& dysses; for-þi sall þou despyse þe wele-fare of þis worlde, þat
þou be noghte þer-with dessayued; and þat leres þe þe gaste of
cunnynge; and þou sall stallworthly suffire tribulacyon, þat
þou be noghte ouercommen; and þat teches vs þe gaste of
stallworthenes. And þire foure suffice till þe lyfe þat es callid
actyfe. And þe toþer thre fallys to þe lyfe þat es callid con-
templatyfe, † For thre maners of contemplacion. Ane es in
creaturs; and þat leres þe gaste of vndirstandynge. The toþer
es in Haly Writte, whare þou sese whatte þou doo & what þou
sall lefe, and þat leres þe the gaste of consaile. The thirde
manere es in Godde Hym-selfe; and þat leres vs þe gaste of
wysdom. Now þou sese thurgh þe gyftes of Ihesu, how He es
besy abowte oure hele.   Eftire þis sall þou wiete whilke ere

X. þe ten comandementis. ¶ Þe firste comandement es þis, 'Thow
sall wirchippe bot a Godde, þi Lorde, and till Hym anely þou
sall serue.' Þat es at say, wyrchipe Hym with righte trouthe,
Serue vntill anely with gude werkes. Here sall þou thynke
if þou hafe lelly serued Godde & wirchiped Godde; if þou hafe
seruede Hym ouer all thynge, if þou hafe ȝolden Hym þat that
þou hyghte, or if þou hafe done lesse penance, and if þou hafe
ȝoldyn Hym þat that þou hyghte Hym in þi cristyndom, That
was, to forsake þe deuelle and all his werkes, and in God lelly
to trowe. And thurghe þis commandement es man ordaynede
ynence God þe Fadire. ¶ Þe toþer commandement es defendid to
take Goddes name in vayne; and lying and falsenes þare-in es
defendid'; and thurghe þis commandement es man ordaynede
ynence Godd' þe Son, þat saise Hym-selfe 'I am sothefastnes.'
¶ Þe thirde commandemente es, 'vmbythynke þe þat þou kepe
þe haly-dayes,' þat es to saye, in þine awen herte, to kepe þe
in riste and pees with-owtten seruage of syn or of bodyly

dedis. And þis commandement ordaynes man to reschayfe
þe Haly Gaste. Þise thre commandmentes lerres man how- *These three as to God.*
gates he sall hafe hym ynence Godd' þe Trynite, to whas lyknes
4 he es made in saule. Þe oþer seuen commandementes leres *The other seven as*
man how he sall hafe hym ynence his euencristen. ¶ Þe firste *to fellow-Christians.*
es, 'þou sall honour þi fadire and þi modire fleschely and *The fourth Command-*
gastely, and þat in twa maners, þat es to say, þat þou be *ment (5th of Decalogue).*
8 bouxom to thaym in reuerence and honcur, and þou helpe þam
at thy powere in all thynges þat þay hafe myster, þat þou be
of lange lyfe in erthe; For if þou will be of lange lyfe, it es
reson þat þou honoure thaym of whaym þou hase þe lyfe; For
12 he þat will noghte honoure hym thurgh whaym he es, it es
noghte righte þat he be mare þan he es. ¶ Þe toþer commande- *The fifth Command-*
ment es þis, 'Þou sall sla na man.' Here sall þou wyt þat *ment (6th of Decalogue).*
slaughter es of many maneres. For þer es manes-slaghter of
16 hand, of tunge, of herte. Mannes-slaynge of hande es when
a man slaes anoþer with his handez, or when he duse hym in
bandis of dede, als in preson or in oþer stede þat may be
encheson of his dede. Manes-slaynge of tunge es in twa
20 maners, thurghe commandement, or thurghe enticement.
Manes-slayng of herte es alswa one twa maners, þat es, when [† lf. 201 bk.]
men ȝernys and couaytes ded of oþer, and when he suffyrs man
to dy, † and will noghte delyuer hym if he hafe powere. ¶ Þe *The sixth Command-*
24 thirde commandement es þis: 'Þou sall do na lechery;' and *ment (7th of Decalogue).*
þat es ryghte. Wha-sa will hafe þe lyfe with-owtten corupcyone
in þe Ioy of heuen, hym byhoues kepe his lyfe þat es dedly,
with-owtten corupcione of body. ¶ The ferthe commandement *The seventh Command-*
28 es þis, 'Þou sall do na thyfte ne na falsenes;' and þat es ryghte. *ment (8th of Decalogue).*
For he þat will safe oþer menes lyfe, he sall noghte do away þat
that moghte his lyfe sustayne. ¶ The fyfte commandement es *The eighth Command-*
þis, 'Þou sall noghte bere false wittnes agaynes thyne euen- *ment (9th of Decalogue).*
32 cristyn with hym þat will noye hym or sla hym.' And þat es
ryghte; For he þat will noghte sckathe his euencristyn, he
sall noghte consente, ne na consaile gyffe, to do hym ill. ¶ Þe *The ninth and tenth*
sexte commandement and þe seuend' er þir, 'Þou sall noghte *Command-ments (10th*
36 couaite þi neghtboure wyfe, ne þou sall noghte couaite his *of Decalogue).*

house, ne nane of his gude wrangwysly,' For he þat hase
wykked wiȝȝ and iȝȝ Entente in his herte, he may noghte lang
with-haldynge hym fra wykkide dede; and þer-fore, if þou wiȝȝ
noghte do lecherye, þou saȝȝ noghte consente to man ne to
woman þat it duse; and if þou wiȝȝ noghte stele, þou saȝȝ
noghte couayte oþer mennes thynges in þi herte. Dere frende,
þir are þe ten commandementes þat God gafe tiȝȝ Moyses in the
mounte of Synay. The thre fyrste er pertenande to þe lufe of
God, and the toþer seuen to þe lufe of þi-selfe and of thyne
euen crystyn.

XI. Now, efter, saȝȝ þou wyt whilke ere þe seuen vertusȝ, þat es to
saye ¶ Trouthe, Trayste, and lufe, Wysedom and Rightwysenes,
Mesure and Force. Of þe same matire er þe seuen vertus þat
þe ten commandementis, bot þis es þe varyance be-twyx thaym:
The ten commandmentis kennes vs what we saȝȝ do, and þe
seuen vertus kennes vs how we saȝȝ doo. The thre fyrste, þat
es to say, Trouthe, trayste and lufe, ordaynes the how þou
saȝȝ lyfe als to Godd': þe toþer foure how þou saȝȝ ordayne thyne
awen lyfe þat saȝȝ lede till þe Ioye of heuen. Dere frende,
the awe to wyt þat we ere aȝȝ made for ane End', þat es to say,
for to knawe Godde, to hafe Hym, and to lufe Hym. Bot thre
thynges er nedefuȝȝ at puruaye tiȝȝ oure cunnynge, That es to
wyte, whedyr we saȝȝ ga, and þat we wyȝȝ comme thedyre, and
þat we hafe trayste to com thedyre; For grete foly ware it to
be-gyn þe thynge mane may noghte ende; ȝitte, one þe toþer
syde, þe mane þat wiȝȝ wyele doo, hym nedide to hafe wysdom,
myghte, and wiȝȝ; þat es to say, þat he konn doo, and þat he
XII. may doo, and þat he wyȝȝ doo. Bot for-þi þat we hafe noghte
cunnynge, myghte, ne wiȝȝ of oure selfe, for-þi hase Godde gyfen
vs trouthe, for to fulfiȝȝ þe defaute of oure myghte. Sothefaste
lufe es for to ordayne oure wiȝȝ to þe tane and to þe toþer.
Trouthe ordaynes vs to Godde þe Son, to whaym es appropyrde
Wysdom; Trayste, tiȝȝ Godd' þe Fadyre, to whaym es appropyrde
myghte; Lufe, to þe Haly Gaste, tiȝȝ whaym es appropyrde
gudnes. And þare trouthe makes vs to hafe knawynge; and
þat knaweynge vs sayse þat He es wondyrfuȝȝ; Fre es He þat

II. St. Edmund's Mirror. Twelve Articles of the Creed.

one þis manere and þus largely gyffes of His gudnes; and of þat comes trayste, and [of] þat knawynge, þat sais þat He es gude Commes þe thyrde Sothefastnes, þat es lufe, For ylke a thynge luffes kyndely þe gude.

† Dere frende, here sall þou wyte whilke are þe twelue artycles of þe trouthe. ¶ The firste es þis, þat Godde es ane in Hym-selfe and thre in persouns, with-owtten begynnynge, and with-owtten Endynge, and þat all thynges [were] made of noghte with His worde. ¶ Þe toþer artecle es, þat Goddes son tuke flesche and blode of þe blyssed mayden Marie, and was borne of hire, sothefaste Godd' and sothefaste man. ¶ Þe thirde es, þat He was dede and grauen, noghte for nede, Bot for to by vs of His fre will. ¶ The ferthe artecle es, þat þe same Ihesu rase fra dede to lyfe, and we sall ryse alswa. ¶ The fyfte artecle es, þat þe same Sothefaste God and man, steighe vp in till heuen in manhed and godhede; and we sall steighe vp alswa thurgh His grace. ¶ Þe sext artecle es baptymme, þat mase man clene of syn þat he drawes of kynde, and gyffes grace to clense. ¶ The Seuend' artecle es confirmacion, þat confermys þe Haly Gaste one man þat es cristenede. ¶ Þe aughtened artecle es penance, þat duse awaye all maner of syn dedly and venyall. ¶ Þe nynde es þe Sacrament of þe Auter, þat confermys þe penance, and gyffes hym force þat he fall noghte efte in syn, and vphaldes hym and reconsailles hym. ¶ Þe tend' artecle es Ordyre, þat gyffes powere till þaym þat are ordeynede to do þaire Offece and to do þe sacramentis. ¶ Þe elleuend' artecle es Matrimone, þat defendis dedly syn in werke of generacyon by-twyx man and woman. ¶ Þe twelfed artecle es Enoyntynge, þat men enoyntes þe seke in perell of dede, for alegeance of body and saule.

¶ Dere frende, aftyre sall þou wyt whilke are þe foure vertus cardynalles, thurgh whilke all manes lyfe es gouernede in þis worlde, þat es, ¶ Cunnynge and Rightwisnes, Force and Mesure. Of thir foure, saise þe Haly Gaste in þe buke of Wysdom, þat þare es na thynge mare profytabill till man in erthe; and so nowe, whare-fore, wha-sa walde any thynge wele do, firste hym byhouys þat he konn chese þe ill fra þe gude, and of twa gude, chese

XIII. [† leaf 202.] The twelve Articles of the Creed.
(1) God.
(2) Christ.
(3) His Death.
(4) His Resurrection.
(5) His Ascension.

XIV. (6) Baptism.
(7) Confirmation.
(8) Penance.
(9) The Eucharist.
(10) Orders.
(11) Matrimony.
(12) Extreme Unction.

XV. The four Cardinal Virtues:
(1) Wisdom.
(2) Righteousness.
(3) Force.
(4) Temperance.

Prudence. þe bettire and leffe þe lesse gude; and þis es the vertu þat es callede ryghtwysnes[1]. And for-þi þat twa thynges lettes man to do wele and lefe þe yll, þat es at say, wele-fare of þis worlde, for it dessayfes hym with false vanytes; þe toþer es tribulacyon, to putt hym down with many scharpnes: agaynes wele-fare sall þou
Temperance. hafe mesure, þat þow be noghte ouer hye. And þis vertu es
Fortitude. called 'temperance.' And agayne aduersyte sall þou hafe 'hardynes,' þat þou be noghte casten downne. And þat vertue es callyde Force or strenghe.

XVI.

vij opera misericordie.

The Seven Works of Mercy.

[† leaf 202 bk.]

How those that are 'in religion' can perform these.

¶ Here-eftyre sall þou wyte whylke are þe seuen werkes of mercy. ¶ **The** firste werke of Mercy es, to gyffe mete to þe hunngry. The toþer es, to gyffe drynke to þe thrysty. The thirde es, to clethe þe nakede. Þe ferthe es, to herbere þe herberles. Þe fyfte es, to vesete þam þat ere in prisonne. † Þe sexte es, to comforth þe seke. The Seuend, to bery þe dede. Thyse are þe seuen werkes of mercy þat are langande to þe body. Bot nowe may þou say to me, 'how sulde I, þat es in Relygyon, and noghte hase to gyffe at ete ne at drynke, ne clathes to þe nakede, ne herbery to þe herberles, For I am at oþer mens will, and noghte at myn awen? For-thi ware it better þat I ware seculere, þat I myghte do þise werkes of mercy.' A, dere frende, be noghte begylede! Better it es to hafe pete and compassione in þi herte of hym þat hase mysese and wrechednes, Thane þou hade all þis werlde to gyffe for charyte; For it es bettir wyth compassion to gyffe þi-selfe als þou erte, þan it es to gyffe þat that þou hase. There-fore, dere frende, gyffe thi-selfe; and þan gyffes þou mare þan es in all þis worlde. Bot now may þou Say me one þis manere:—'Sothe it es þat it es better to gyffe hym-selfe þan it es to gyffe of his, bot better es þe tane and þe toþer þan es ane be it selfe, for lesse es a gud

The blessedness of poverty.

þan twa.' It es noghte swa: For whethire es better be callede Godde, or His seruande. Thow wate wele þat es better to be callede Godd. Bot þase þat suffirs hunngere, thryste, caulde and defaute, and oþer wrechidnes and mysese, calles oure Lorde

---

[1] The description of the virtue of Prudence is here given to Righteousness or Justice, the account of which is omitted.

II. St. Edmund's Mirror. Riches and Poverty. 31

Ihesu Criste Hym-selfe; For He saise þus in þe Gosepelle, 'What als þou dyde to þe leste of myñ, þou did to me.' Saynt Barnarde says, 'Thire pure hase noghte in erthe, ne thire riche
4 hase noghte in heueñ; and þare-fore, if þe Riche will it hafe, thaym byhoues bye it at þe pure.' Now wate I wele þou couaytes to wyte whilke are verray pure, and whilke noghte. Now *Who are the really poor.* herkeñ with deuocyoñ. Suṁ are þat hase reches and lufes
8 thaym, and þase are þe haldande and þe couaytourse of þis worlde. Othere are þat hase þaṁ noghte, bot thay luffe thayṁ, and thay walde hafe thayṁ gladly; and þase are þe wrechide beggers of þe worlde, and þe false folke in religyoñ, and þase
12 are als riche and richere þaṁ þe oþer. And of thaṁ Ihesu saise in þe gospelle þat 'lyghtere it ware a camelle to passe thurghe a nedill eghe, þan þe riche to coṁ in-to þe blysse of heueñ.' Suṁ are þat hase reches, bot thay lufe thaym noghte; Noghte *Those to whom riches*
16 for-thy þay will wele hafe þaṁ; and þase are þe gud meñ of *are a blessing.* þe worlde þat dispendis wele that at þay hafe. Bot fone are of þase. Ȝit it are oþer þat hase noghte reches, ne lufes noghte thaym, ne will noght hafe þaṁ; and þase are þe gude folke þat
20 are in religioñ and þase are sothefastly pure; and þairs es þe Ioye of heueñ, For þat es the benysoñ of þe pure. Than it behufes þat þe riche hafe þe reuere of þat benysoñ; and þarefore may I say, 'Blyssede be þe pouer, for þaires es þe kyngdoṁ and þe
24 Ioye of heueñ.' And swa may I say of þe riche, For þairs es pyne of helle. Alswa pouer þay are þat hase pouerte and lufes na reches; and pouer þay are þat hase reches and lufes pouert.

¶ Now aftire þis, awe þe to wyte whylke are þe seueñ XVII.
28 prayers of þe *Pater noster*, þat duse away all ill and purchase all *The seven prayers of the* gude. And þase seueñ prayers er contende in þe *Pater noster*, *Pater Noster.* þe whilke oure Lorde Ihesu Criste kennde till His discyples, how þay [suld] pray Godd þe Fadire, and said thaym one þis
32 manere, 'Wheñ ȝe † sall praye, one þis wyese sall ȝe say, *Pater* [† leaf 203.] *noster qui es in celis, &c.*' Now, my frende, wit þou þat oure Lorde Ihesu Cryste kennes vs in þe gospelle to make þis prayere. And þare-fore I walde at þou wyste at þe begynnynge
36 whate es prayere or orysone, and sythyñ þat þou vndirstande

II. St. Edmund's Mirror. The Fatherhood of God.

What Prayer is.

þe prayere of þe *pater noster*. Prayere or Oryson es noghte elles bot ȝernyng of saule, with certayne trayste þat it commes þat þou prayes. And in þat trayste vs settis Ihesu Criste when He kennes vs to call Godde oure fadyre þat es in heuen, For in Hym sall man hafe certayne trayste þat He may and will all gudnes gyffe þat oure saule kan ȝerne, and mekill mare; þe whilke es betakynde by þise wordes, *Qui es in celis*, þat es to say, þe whilke es in heuen. For if Godde will call Hym-selfe oure fadyre, þan He makes vs to wiet þat He lufes vs als childyre, and at He will gyfe us all þat we hafe myster of. Bot certanly if all þe lufe þat euer had fadire or modire vn-to þaire childyre, or all othire lufes of þis worlde ware gedirde to-gedyre in a lufe, and ȝit þat lufe ware multipliede als mekill als mans herte moghte thynke, ȝit it moghte na thynge atteyne to þe lufe þat Godde oure fadyre hase vn-till vs, þare whare we are hys enmys. And þat sall we wele see thurgh þe grace of Godde, If we se one what manere He is oure Fadyr, and what He has don for vs. Wit þou, þat when God made all creaturs of noghte, we rede noghte þat He made any creature till His lyknes bot man allanne; and þare-fore Godd He es, and makere of all thynges of þe worlde, Bot He es noghte þaire fadyre; Bot vn-till vs, thurghe His awen myghte full of mercy, es He Godd and makere and Fadyr, For þat our saule es lelly lyke vn-till þe lyknes of þe Fadyr, and þe Son, and þe Haly Gaste, þat ere hallyly a Godd' and persons thre. And all þis werlde He hase made to serue man, whils mane will duelle in His lele lufe als His awen childyre. Bot als tyte als we twyn fra þat lele lufe, for lufe of þis lyfe, or for any oþer thynge, we losse þe lordechipe of þis worlde, and becommes thralles drerryly to þe deuelle, þare we ware be-fore fre, and ayers of þe erytage of þe kyngdom of heuen, and to welde þe welthe of þis werlde. Allas may saye, Allas! Allas! what here es a sorowfull chaunge whasa it vndyrstode! Wit þou wele þat here es gret lykynge of lufe, when Godd þat es with-owttyn begynnynge, and es withowtten chaungeyng, and duellys with-owttyn Endynge, for He es al-þir-myghtyeste and alþirwyseste, and alswa alþire-beste

God, our Father.

He made man alone in His likeness.

God's great mercy in our Creation.

þat mannes herte may noghte thynke, in whaym es lufe and
Ioy endles, here, I say, es takyn of gret lufe, þat He deyned Hym *God made us in His own*
to make vs till His awen lyknes righte als we had bene His *likeness,*
though He
4 awen chosen childyre, and moghte hafe lefte vs to be a littill vyle *might have*
made us like
matire als we ware made of oure modyr, þat vile es to neuen ; *beasts.*
or He moghte hafe made vs at His will anykyn oþer bestis; and
þan had we dyede to-gedire, bathe body and saule. Bot when
8 He hade made vs man, and gafe † vs þe saule to His awen [† leaf 203 bk.]
lyknes, (louede and luffede be þat Lorde !) for to be ayers of þe
Erytage of heuen and lyfe in þat gret Ioye with-owtten Ende,
Now es na herte sa herde þat it na moghte nesche, and lufe *So our hearts*
ought to
12 Swylke a Godd with all his myghte. And his herte suld melte, *soften, and to love Him.*
filled of Ioy, if it thoghte sothely of þat grace þat oure Lorde
hase don till vs by-fore all oþer creaturs. And ȝitt did He mare
thurghe His mekill mercy ; For, whene we ware, thurghe oure *And when we were thralls to*
16 Sorowfull syn, twynnede fra Godd, oure Sweteste Fadire, and *the evil spirit, He sent His*
become thralles to þe ill gaste, Than He, thurghe His maste *own Son to*
mercy, Sente His awen Sonne, þat with Hym es Godd in His Godhede, for to take flesche and blode of þe Virgyn Marie, Mayden
20 and modyr, lastand in Ioy ; and one þis manere did He þe dede.
In state of thralle tuke He oure flesche to suffre þe gylteste *take our flesh*
and die for us
pouerte, and schame, and noyes, and paynnes, þat neuer dyd ill
ne na maner of syn, and Sythen delyuerde Hym till þe vileste
24 dede, and þe schamefulleste þat man moghte thynke, to delyuer
vs wreches of sorowfull handis, and of þe pynand preson puttid
in hell, and to make vs to comme till þe heghe heuen, whare *and lift us to*
high heaven
we sall be als kynges corounde in blyse, if we do þe will of þat *and to be*
kings in
28 swet Lorde, þat for vs ordeynede Hym to dye one þe crosse als *bliss.*
þofe He had benne a wykkid thefe. Dere Frende, nowe hase
þou here twa thyngez in þe whilke Godde hase schewede vs þat
He es oure fadire, and þat He lufes vs als His awen childyre þare
32 we are agayne Hym with oure wykked syn. The firste es, þat
He made vs till His awen lyknes ; and þe toþer es, þat He boghte
vs fra presoun with His precyouse dede of His manhede. For
þe fyrste, es man halden till Hym, for to lufe Hym with all his
36 herte. Bot þan may þou aske, ' what sall I do Hym for þe toþer *What services*

can we render unto God for His goodness?

thynge? For if I sall with pouerhede lofe Godd' þe Fadyr, and lufe Hym and serue Him with all my saule and with all my herte in all thynges, for-þi þat He made me of noghte and gafe me saule aftir His awen lyknes,—als it was commandyd in þe alde lawe be-fore Godde was borne and be-com man for vs,— what moghte I now do Hym, when He, for me wrechid synnere, sa mekill Hym lawede þat He walde becomme man, and He gafe Hym to me, when He, thurghe His sweteste mercy, walde dye for me, and of þe maste noyouse and þe moste vile dede þat

We cannot repay Him for His mercy.

euer was thoghte? I wate neuer what I may say here; For if I myghte lyffe a hundrethe ȝere, and if I moghte in þat tym, ilk a day at a tym, dye als vile ded als He for me dide, ȝit ne ware it noghte ynence His gret gyftez, when He es sothely said Goddes Sonne of heuen, and gaffe Hym selfe till vs, þat tynte was for syn thurgh, and put in to þe pyne of helle, and þare, in þe dispytte of Hym, seruede to þe deuelle. How sulde we þan ȝelde Hym þe gude gret gyfte, when He walde sende His awen Sone to be pynede for oure syn?'

God only requires of us contrition and humility. [† leaf 204.]

Now I sall lere the, if God gyffe me grace, how oure dere Fadir askes nane oþer store bot that we, with herte, knawe oure awen Febillnes and oure wrechidnes, þat we hafe for oure awen syn. † Thane sall we be in bitternes of penance, and crye till Hym faste mercy, þat He vs saue for His haly name, For of oure selfe hafe we noghte Hym for to ȝelde; þare-fore said the prophete in þe psalme, **Quid retribuam Domino pro omnibus que retribuit**[1] **michi? Calicem salutaris accipiam, et nomen Domini invocabo,** *etc'.* þat es, ' what sall I ȝelde to God for all His gud gyftes þat He me gyffes als Lorde, with-owtten my deserte? The coppe of hele I sall take, and calle þe name of my lorde.' The cope of hele whare-of dranke oure Lord Ihesu oure Saueour, þat es, the bytternes of þe penance in His grete pynes, and þat man in all his thoghtez calles Godez name, þat sothefastly knawes þat he hase noghte of hym-selfe bot sorowe and synne.

The more we feel weak the humbler we shall be.

And wit thou þat, if sothefastenes be sett faste in thi saule, þe mare þat þou knawes þe for wrechide and febyll, þe mare sall þou

[1] MS. *retrebuit.*

II. St. Edmund's Mirror. The Duty of Brotherly Love.

meke þe, and calle on Hys mercy. And þus it was of oure swete
Lady, mayden and modyr; For scho had mare of grace þane *Such humility and meekness*
any in this lyfe, man or woman þat euer was borne, Thare-fore *as was in our Lady, should*
4 scho halde hir lesse and lawere þan any oþer wyghte, and mare *we have.*
cryede scho mercy þan any oþer man, when sothefaste Goddes
Son lighte in hir wambe. My dere frende, se now aftir-warde
why oure Lord Ihesu kennes vs in þe Gospelle to saye ' oure *What is implied by*
8 Fadire,' and noghte ' my Fadir'; For by þat will He kenn vs þat *Our Father?*
we suld gedyre all men with vs in oure prayers, For all ere oure
brethire, crystende and vncristend' men, For þat all of a gouernaylle hafe we a Fadyr. And þat þou may þis thynge, thurghe
12 þe grace of Godd, clerelyere See, Gyffe gude Entente till þat at
I say. Hym calles þou 'thi fleschely broþer,' þat hase his body
of þe same man and woman of whaym þou hase thyne. Thane
sall þou wele halde hym þi broþer þat hase his saule of þe Same
16 fadir of heuen of whaym þou hase þi saule, and of swylke
a kynd, and of swylke a lyknes; For als wele made Godd ilke
man till lyknes of þe Trinyte als He did þe. And þis broþer- *The duty of brotherly*
hede mare suld we lufe, and mare dere halde, þan þe broþerhede *love.*
20 of þe flesche, in als mekill als þe saule es mare nobyll þan þe
flesche, and in als mekill als Godd, oure fadir, of heuen, es
mare nobill, and mare for to lufe, þan oure fleschly fadir. And
þat suld we do if we saghe als clerely with oure gastely eghe
24 als we do with oure bodyly eghe. Bot for-thy þat we see
noghte bot with þe fleschely eghe, als it ware bestes, we hafe
na knawynge ne na lufe bot of þat broþerhede þat commes of
þe flesche stynkande and foule. **Allas**! Allas! what sorowfull
28 thynge thus hase blyndid vs! Certis, na thynge mare blyndis
manes saule þane lufe of erthely thynge þat sonne takes ende.
For-þi behufes man lefe his propire will, if he will perfitly
knawe þe lufe-somest broþerhede. Whare-of now mekill I hafe
32 spoken, For whate-sa-euer we hafe in body or in saule of
gudnes or of †fayrenes, we hafe it of oure fadyr of heuen, [† leaf 204 bk.]
Godd, þat es till vs fadir, and Euenly till all His creaturs, noghte *God the lov-*
anely for His makynge of noghte, ne for His gouernyng of His *ing Father of all His*
36 grace, for His purchasynge þat He made of vs þat ware tynt *creatures.*

childir, with His flesche and His blode þat He for vs gafe, als
Saynt Austyn þe nobill clerke witnes. He sayse 'þe Fadir
gaffe His Son, thurgh whaym He walde by vs thralles; He gafe
þe Haly Gaste, thurgh whaym He walde purchase þe thralles 4
in His childire. Þe Sonn, He gafe in pryse of raunson; þe
Haly Gaste, in preuelege of purchase; and þar-fore þe Fadir
kepis Hym selfe in Erytage till His childir þat He purchase[d].'
And þarefore, dere frende, na man sall mystrayste of þe lufe 8
of His swete Fadirhede, and of His dere pete; For mare es His
mercy þan all oure wykkednes; For wha sa calles till Hym
with all his herte, with-owtten faile He will here hym, for He
es full of mercy. And þare-fore, als I be-fore saide, with ȝernynge 12
of saule and certayne trayste, calle apon Hym trewely with all
thi herte. He es þi Fadir pereles, þat purchacecez þe pees;
and saye traystely till Hym als Hym-selfe vs lerede, *Pater noster
qui es in celis*, þat es to say, Oure Fadir that es in heuen; 16
sanctificetur nomen tuum, þat es to say, halyed be þi name;
adveniat regnum tuum, it com, þi kyngedom; *Fiat voluntas
tua, sicut in celo et in terrâ*, þi will be donne, swa in erthe als it
es in heuen; *panem nostrum cotidianum da nobis hodie*, Oure 20
ylke day brede þou gyffe vs to day; *Et dimitte nobis debita
nostra, sicut et nos dimittimus debitoribus nostris*, and forgyffe
vs oure dettis als we forgyffe our dettours; *Et ne nos inducas
in temptacionem*, and suffire vs noghte be ledde in-to fandyngis, 24
Set libera nos a malo, bot delyuer vs fra all ill thynges *Amen*!
Þat es to say, Swa mot it be! Now, my dere frende, þou sall
wyt þat þis Oryson passes all oþer prayers, pryncypally in twa
thynges, þat es to say, in worthynes and in profyte. In 28
worthynes, for þat God Hym-selfe mad it; and for-þi do þay gret
schame and gret vnreuerence till Ihesu, Goddes Son, þat takes
þam till wordis rynnand and curius, and leues þe prayere þat
He vs kennede, þat wate all þe will of Godd' þe Fadir, and þe 32
whilke orysone commes mare till His plesynge, and whate
thynges þe wrechede caytyfe hase myster at pray fore. Alswa,
als I hafe sayde, He wate anely all þe Fadir wyll, and He
wate all oure nede; and þare-fore a hundrethe thousande er 36

II. St. Edmund's Mirror. Fullness of the Paternoster.

dyssayued with multyplicatione of wordes and of orysouns;
For, when þay wene þat þay hafe grete deuocyon, þan hafe þai
a fulle fleschely lykynge, For-thy þat ilk a fleschely lykynge
4 delytes þam kyndely in swylke turnede langage; and þare-fore *Don't delight in polisht phrases and rymes.*
I walde þat þou war warre, For I say þe sykerly, þat it es a
foule lychery for to delyte þe in rymmes and slyke gulyardy;
ȝit one a-noþer syde, Saynt Austyne, and Saynt Gregore, and
8 oþer halowes þat prayede als was þaire lykynge. I blame *Those who leave the Lord's Prayer for others are to blame*
noghte prayers, bot I blame þase þat lefes þe prayere of Godd
þat Hym-selfe made, and lerede vs for to pray, þat es, *Pater noster,*
and takes þam till þe Orysons of a synfull Saynte whare þay
12 fynde it wretten, For oure Lorde Ihesus Hym-selfe sayse in the
† gospell, 'when ȝe will praye, prayes noghte with many [† leaf 205.]
wordes, bot praye one þis manere, *Pater noster &c'.'*

¶ Dere frende, ȝit sall þou wit one anoþer syde þat þe *Pater* *The Lord's Prayer contains all things which we need to ask.*
16 *noster* passes all oþer prayers in worthynes; For þare-in es
contende all thyngez what-sa we hafe myster of, till þis lyfe
or till þe toþer. For we praye þare-in Godd' þe Fadyr, þat
He delyuer vs of all illes, and þat He gyffe vs all gudes, and
20 þat He make vs swylke þat we may neuer do ill, ne þat we may
noghte fayle of gude. And now, all þe ille þat vs greues,
ouþer es it, ille þat es donne, or it es ille for to com, or elles it
es ille þat we suffire nowe. Of þat ille þat es donne and *How we pray to be deliv-ered from evil.*
24 passede, we praye oure swete Lorde þat He delyuer vs þer-of,
when we say *Dimitte nobis debita nostra, etc'*. We pray Hym
delyuer vs of ill þat es for to com, when we say *et ne nos*
inducas in temptacionem. Of illes þat we suffire nowe, we
28 praye Hym þat He delyuer vs, when we say *Set libera nos*
a malo. ¶ Ȝit, dere Frende, on a oþer syde, wit þou þat all *How we pray for good.*
maner of gude þat es, Ouþer it es erthely gude, or gastely gude,
or gude lastande endles. For erthely gude we praye, when we
32 saye *Panem nostrum cotidianum da nobis hodie*; For gastely
gude we praye, when we say *Fiat voluntas tua, sicut in celo et in*
terra; For endles gude we praye, when we say *Adveniat regnum*
tuum; and confermyng of all this we praye, when we say
36 *Sanctificetur nomen tuum*.

¶ Now, my dere frende, þese ere seuen prayers of þe Ewangelle þat oure Lorde Ihesu Criste kenned till His dyscypills. And þou sall wit þat þese foure wordes þat comes be-fore, þat es to wit, *Pater noster qui es in celis*, leres vs how we sall praye, 4 and what oure selfe sall be in prayere; For we sall, in ylke ane Oryson, haue foure thynges, þat es to say, perfite lufe till Hym till whaym we praye, and certayne trayste to haue þat at we praye fore, and stabill trouth in Hym in whaym we trowe, 8 and sothefaste mekenes of þat, that of oure selfe, na gude we haue. Perfite lufe es vndirstanden in þis worde *Pater*, For ylke a creature kyndly lufes his Fadir. Certayne trayst es contende in þis worde *noster*; For if He be ours, þan may 12 we sekerly trayst in Hym þat He es halden till vs. Stabill trouthe es taken in þise wordes *Qui es*; For when we say *qui es*, þan graunt we wele þat Godd es þat we neuer sawe; and þat es ryghte trouthe, For trouthe es na noþer thyng bot 16 trowyng of thyng þat may noghte be sene. Sothefaste mekenes es betakynde in þis worde *In celis*, For when we thynke how He es heghe in Ioy, and how we are here lawe in besynes, than we are mekide. Bot when we hafe festenede þere foure thynges 20 in oure hertes, þan may we hardyly praye, and saye with all oure affeccyon, *Sanctificetur nomen tuum*, þat es to say, 'haly be thi name!' als swa stabill þi name, þat es, Fadir, in vs, þat we be one þat manere þi childire þat we do na thyng þat 24 be agaynes þi will, and that euer-mare we doo þat at commes to þi plesyng, thurgh grauntynge of þi grace. And for-thi þat we may noghte euer-mare do þat perfitely whyls we ere in þis caytifede worlde, þare-fore pray we þus, and sayse, *Adveniat* 28 *regnum tuum*, þat es to say, it com till vs, þi kyngdom, þat we regne in þe, Ihesu, in þis lyfe thurgh thi grace, and þou in vs in þe toþer lyfe thurgh Ioy. And þis ilke we praye for þase þat are in purgatorie; and for-þi þat we neuer-mare may hafe 32 †parte with Ioye of heuen if we do noghte thi will in erthe, þare-fore we praye thus, *Fiat voluntas tua, sicut in celo et in terra*, þat es to say, thi will be done, als in heuen, swa in erthe. Alswa say 'make vs to do þi wyll,' þat es to say, þou gyffe 36

vs grace to do all þat þou commandes, and to lefe all þat þou
defendis, and þat swa in erthe als in heueñ, þat es to say,
als Michaelle, and Gabrielle, and Raphaelle, Cherubyñ and
4 Seraphyñ, and all þe oþer angells and archangells, and all þase
þat are Ordeynede to þe endles lyfe in Ioy, in ilke a kynde,
in ilke ane ordire, and in ilke ane elde, thi wille duse; and
for-thi þat we may noghte do þi will whills we lyffe in þis body,
8 if þou ne sustayne vs noghte, þare-fore say we þus, *Panem* ‘Give us this day our daily bread.’
nostrum cotidianum da nobis hodie, þat es to say, Oure ilke
day brede þou gyffe vs to-day; als swa say ‘þou gyffe vs Force in
body and in saule, and hele, if it be þi will, of þe tane and offe
12 þe toþer.’ And here es for to wit, þat þare es thre maners of
brede, þat es, bodyly brede, þat es to say, Fode and clethynge;
þare es brede gastely, þat es to say, of haly wrytte þe leryng;
and þare es þe brede of Eukaryste, þat es þe grace in þe
16 sacrament of þe autere, for to comforthe þe kynde of þe tane
and þe toþer.

Bot for-thi þat we ere worthi na gudnes whills we ere
bowndeñ in synñ, þare-fore say we þus, *Dimitte nobis debita* ‘Forgive us our tres-
20 *nostra, sicut et nos dimittimus debitoribus nostris*, þis es to say, passes, as we forgive them
‘Forgyffe vs oure dettis als we forgyffe oure dettours.’ þou sall that trespass against us.’
wyt þare oure synns byndis oure dettours to pynne; þare-fore
we pray Ihesu to for-gyff vs synnes, þat es to say, all þat we
24 hafe synnede in thoghte, in worde and in dede; and þat ryghte
als we for-gyffe till þase þat hase mysdone agaynes vs. And
for-þi þat a lyttill vs helpes to hafe forgyfnes of syñ, if we may
noghte kepe vs fra syñ, þare-fore pray we þus, *Et ne nos inducas* ‘Lead us not into tempta-
28 *in temptacionem*, and þis es to say, ‘lede us noȝte in-to na tion,’
fandyngis, als swa say, Suffere vs noghte be ouer-commeñ in
fandyngez of þe deuell, ne of þe flesch, ne of þe werlde. And
noghte allanly we pray þat we be delyuered of all euyll
32 fandyngez, Bot alswa we pray þat we be delyuered of all ill
thyngis, wheñ we say, *Set libera nos a malo*; and þis es to say, ‘But deliver us from evil.’
‘Bot delyuer vs of all ill thyngis,’ þat es, of body and of saule,
of syñ and of pyne, For syñ that now es or sall be. Say we
36 Amen! þat es to say, ‘swa be it!’ and for-thi sayse oure Lorde

II. St. Edmund's Mirror. Lord's Prayer: Heaven.

Ihesu Criste in þe gospelle, 'What sa þou prayes my fadir in my name, He sall do it;' and þer-fore say at þe Ende, *Per Dominum nostrum Iesum Cristum, filium tuum, &c'*.

When the words are said with the mouth their meaning ought to be thought of in the heart.

And now, my dere frende, vndirstande noghte þat þou sall say þi *Pater noster* with mouthe, als I hafe it here wretyn be-fore þe. Bot say all anely þe nakede lettir with þi mouthe, and thynke in þi herte of this þat I hafe said here, of ilke a worde by it-selfe; and rekk noghte þof þou ne multyply many *Pater nosters*; For it es better to say a *Pater noster* with gude

Devotion the important thing.

deuocyon, þan a thousande with-owtten deuocyon; For þus sais Saynte Paule appertly; he sayse, 'me ware leuer say fyve

[† leaf 206.]

wordes in herte deuotely, þane fyve thousande † with my mouthe with-owtten lykynge.' And one þe same manere sall þou say and do at thyne offece in þe qweire; for swa sayse þe prophete, *Psallite sapienter*; and þat es to say, 'Synges and versy wyesly,' þat es, to say or to syng wyesly, þat es, þat thi herte be one þat at þou saise, and one þat at oþer saise, þat þou here it besyly; For if þi body be at thi seruyce, and þi mouthe speke one a wyse, and thi herte thynke of wrechidnes caytefly,

The mischief of indevout service.

þan es þou twynned'; For when þou swa es twynned, þou tynes þe mede of þi seruyce; For þe awe to serue Godd' with all þi herte, with all þi saule, and with all þi vertu; and swa þou may pay þi Godd. Bot þare es many thynges þat ere cause of swylke wrechede twynnynge, als mete, drynke, Reste, cleythynge, layke, discorde, Thoghte, laboure, hethynge. These makes hippynge, homerynge, of medles momellynge. And þare-fore take kepe what oure Lorde Ihesu Criste saise in þe gospelle: 'Firste,' He saise, 'sekes þe kyngdom of heuen, and all þat 3e hafe myster of sall be gyffen 3owe with-owttyn any askynge.'

XVIII. Thare-fore, dere Frende, þou sall wit what þou sall hafe in þe

The gifts that the faithful shall have in heaven.

blysse of heuen. Wit þou wele þat þou sall hafe Seuen gyftes in body, and Seuen in saule, þat es to say, Fairenes in body with-owttyn fylth, lyghtenes with-owttyn slewth, Force with-owtten Feblesce, Frenes with-owtten thralledome, lykynge with-owtten noye, lufelynes with-owttyn envye, hele with-owttyn sekenes, lange lyfe with-owttyn ende. Thou sall hafe in saule, Wysedome

II. St. Edmund's Mirror. Heaven's Joys. Contemplation.

with-owtten ygnorance, Frenchipe with-owtten hateredyn,
Accorde with-owtten discorde, Myghte with-owtten wayknes,
honour with-owtten dishonour, Sekirnes with-owtten drede,
4 Ioy with-owtten sorowe. Bot þe wreches in helle, all þe *The penalties of hell.*
reuerce, both in body and in saule, þat es to say, Fylth with- *Ills which the wretches in hell shall undergo.*
owttyn fairenes, Slouthe with-owtten lyghtenes, Feblesce
with-owtten force, Thraldom with-owtten freenes, Angwyse
8 with-owtten lykynge, Sekenes with-owtten hele, ded with-
outten ende. Thare sall be in þair saules, Ignorance
with-owttyn Wysdome, hatredyn with-owtten lufe, Discorde
with-owtten Accorde, feblesce with-owtten powere, Schame
12 with-owtten honour, Drede with-owtten sekernes, and Sorowe
with-owtten Ioy. And for þis sall þou seke with all þi
myghte, þat þou may wyn þe Ioye of heuen; For þare es sa
gret Ioye and sa mekill swettnes þat, if þou myghte lyffe fra þe
16 begynnynge of þe worlde vn-till þe ende, and hafe all þe lykynge
þat þou couthe ordeyne, ȝit þou sulde with gret ryghte lefe all
þase for to be a day in þe Ioy of heuen. And thus endys þe *This is sufficient of the second part of contemplation.*
toþer degre of contemplacyone, þat es to say, þe contemplacione
20 of haly writte; of þe whylke, if þou take gud kepe in þi herte,
it sall be lyghte vnto þe, ilke a worde to halde. One ane oþer
syde, if þou hafe mater to speke vn-to þe clerkez, be þay neuer
sa wyse, or to lewede men, be þay neuer so ruyde, of þe clerkes
24 þou mofe som matirs of þis, and alswa at þou may lere more.
And when þou spekes till sympill men, and ruyde, †gladly þou [†leaf 206 bk.]
lere þam with swettnes, For þou hafe enoghe whare-of þou may
speke, and how þou sall þi lyfe amende and gouerne, and oþer
28 menes alswa.

Þe thirde degre of contemplacyon es in Godd' Hym-selfe. XIX.
And þat may be on twa maners, þat es, with-owtten in *The third part of contemplation is of God.*
His manhede, and in His Godhede so blyschede. For þus
32 saise Saynt Austyn, For-þi be-come Godd' man, For to make
mane to Se Godd' in his kynde; For wheþer som he ȝode with-in
or with-owtten, euer-mare moghte man fynde pasture; with-
owtten, thurgh consederacyon of His manhed'; with-in, thurghe
36 contemplacyon of His Godhede. Of His manhede sall þou thynke *The manhood of Christ.*

thre thyngez: þe meknes of His Incarnacyon, þe swetenes of His conuersasion, and þe grete charite of His passione. Bot þis may þou noghte do all att anes; and þare-fore hafe I twynned the thaym by þe Seuen houres of þe daye þat þou saise in þe kyrke, Swa þat nan houre passe the, þat þou ne sall be swetely ocupyed in þi herte. Bot nowe for to do þis, þan sall þou wit þat till ilke ane houre of þe daye es dowbyll medytacyon, ane of His passyon, and anoþer of þe toþer seson. ¶ Now, dere frende, before matyns sall þou thynke of þe swete byrthe of Ihesu Cryste al-þer-fyrste, and sythyn eftyrwarde of His passion. Of His byrth, sall thou thynke besyly þe tym, and þe stede and þe houre, þat oure Lorde Ihesu Criste was borne of His modir Marie. Þe tyme was in myd-wyntter, when it was maste calde; þe houre was at mydnyghte, þe hardeste houre þat es; þe stede was in mydwarde þe strete, in a house with-owtten walles. In clowtis was He wonden, and als a chylde was He bunden; and in a crybbe by-fore ane oxe and ane asse, þat lufely lorde layde was, for þare was na noþer stede voyde. And here sall þou thynke of þe kepynge of Marye, and of hir childe, and of hir spouse Ioseph—wat Ioye Ihesu þam sente. Thou sall thynke also of þe hyrdes þat saw þe takyn of His byrthe; and þou sall thynke of þe swete felachippe of Angells, and rayse vpe thi herte and syng with þam, *Gloria in excelsis Deo, &c.* Of þe passion sall þou thynke how þat He was at swylke a tym of þe nyghte betrayed by His descyple, and taken als a traytoure, and bownden als a thefe, and ledde als a felon.

XXI. ¶ Be-fore pryme þou sall thynke of þe passion of Ihesu and of His Ioyfull ryssynge. Of His passyon sall þou thynke how þe Iewes ledd Hym into þaire counsaile, and bare false wytnes agayne Hym, and put appone Hym þat He had saide blasefeme, þat es, sclandyre in Godd, and þat He had said þat He suld haue distroyede þe temple of Godd, and make agayne anoþer with-in the thirde day; and þan þay bygan to dryfe Hym till hethyng, and to fulle Hym als a fule, and spite one Hym in dispyte in His faire face; and sythyn thay hide His eghen, and gafe Hym bofetes grete, and sythen asked Hym whate He was þat Hym

smate ; and sytheꝺ, þay ledde Hym dreryly to þe dede, † and ȝitt [† leaf 207.]
neue*r* He sayde tiƚƚ thaym anes why þay swa dyde. Many
othyre wykkydnes þay dide Hym, þat lange ware to telle. Ȝitt
4 before pryme saƚƚ þou thynke of þe haly rysesynge, þat at þat
tyme of þe daye Ihe*s*u Ioyfully rase fra dede to lyfe, wheꝺ
þat He hade destruyede helle and delyue*r*ede haly sawles owte
of þe powere of þe deuelle. ¶ Ȝitt before vndrone saƚƚ þou thynke XXII.
8 of þe passioꝺ and of þe witsondaye. Of þe passioꝺ ꭅaƚƚ þou The scourging and giving of
thynke, how þat tyme oure Lorde Ihe*s*u Cryste dispytousely the Spirit before Undroun.
was dispuylede, nakkynde and bowndeꝺ tiƚƚ a tree in Pylate
house, and swa wykkedly scourgede and doungeꝺ, þat of His
12 swete body, fra þe heued tiƚƚ þe fute, noghte was lefte hale. And
at þat ilke houre þou saƚƚ thynke of þe witsonnday, how þe
tyꝳ of þe day oure Lorde Ihe*s*u Criste sente þe Haly Gaste tiƚƚ
His disciples, in liknes of fyre, and of tun*n*ges, in takynnynge
16 þat þay sulde hafe abowndance in worde and brynnynge in lufe,
and þat ryghte es þe *pur*ueance of oure Lorde *pur*uayde ; For
in twa maners þe wykked gaste begylede maꝺ in paradyse, þat
es to saye, wi*th* wykked entycement of his tunge, and wi*th* þe
20 caldnes of his venyꝳ. And for-þi come þe Haly Gaste in
lyknes of tung, agayne þe Entycement of þe deuelle, and in
fyre for to distruye þe caldnes of his venyꝳ. ¶ Be-fore myddaye XXIII.
saƚƚ þou thynke of þe Anu*n*ciacyoꝺ, and of Ihe*s*u passioꝺ. And The Annunciation and
24 of þe Anunciacioꝺ saƚƚ þou thynke of þe grete mercy of oure Crucifixion before midday.
Lorde Ihe*s*u Criste, whi þat He walde be-com*m*e maꝺ, and For
vs suffire þe dede in þat swete manhed Seꝺ He moghte hafe
boghte vs agayne on oþer manere. And þat dyde He for tiƚƚ
28 drawe tiƚƚ Hyꝳ þi luffe. For if ane hade bene þi maker, and
anoþer thi byere, and hade sufferde in thaire bodyes aƚƚ oure
sorowe for to by aƚƚ oure lufe, Than hade noghte oure trouthe
bene anely in ane. Off þe passioꝺ saƚƚ þou thynke at þat houre
32 how oure Lorde Ihe*s*u was done one þe Crosse be-twyx twa
thefes, ane one His ryghte syde, and anoþer one His lefte syde,
and Hym-selfe þay hangede be-twix þaꝳ twa, alls mayste*r* of
thefes. For if all þe sekenes of þis werlde and aƚƚ þe sorowe
36 ware in þe body of a maꝺ anely, and þat man myghte consayfe

alls mekill noye and Angwysce and Sorowe in his body als all
þe men of þis werlde moghte thynke, ȝitt it ware full littill or
ells noghte to regarde of þe sorowe þat He sufferde for vs ane
houre of þe daye. ¶ Before none sall þou thynke of þe passion
and of þe gloriouse Ascencion. Of þe passione sall þou thynke,
þat at swylke a tym of þe daye dyede þe makere of lyfe, for
þi lufe. And here sall þou thynke of þe wordes þat Ihesu
spake on þe crose, and of þe foure takynes þat be-felle in His
dede. The fyrste worde was þis þat He spake, 'Fadire, for-gyffe
þam þis syn, for þay wate noghte whate þay doo.' The toþer
worde was þis, þat He said to þe thefe, 'For sothe I say the, þis
day sall þou be with me in paradyse.' The thirde was þat
He saide to His modire of Sayne John His cosynne, 'Woman,
lo þare thi son!' And to þe discyple saide He, 'Manne, lo þare
thy Modire!' The ferthe worde þat He saide was this, 'Godd,
my Godd, † whi hase þou lefte me þus.' The fyfte was, '*Scicio*,'
þat es to say, 'I haf thriste.' The sexte worde was this,
'*In manus tuas Domine, &c*'. whilke es for to saye, 'Fadir, in-to
þi haundis I gyffe my sawle.' The Seuend worde was þis,
Consummatum est, þat es to say, 'Now es þe prophecye fulfillede,'
and with þat worde He helde His hede downne, and gafe þe
gaste. Now þe takynes þat ware in His dede ere þire. Firste,
all þe erthe by-gane to tremble, and þe vaile of þe temple braste
in twa and felle doun, þe stanes raue in soundire, þe graues
opyned and þe dede men rase, and þe sonne with-drewe his
lyghte fra þe werlde fra myddaye to noune. Of þe Ascencione
sall þou thynke that swylke a tym of þe daye wente vpe oure
Lorde Ihesu Criste in-till þe mounte of Olyuete, Seande His
discyples and His swete modire Marie, how He steighe in-till
heuen, and sett Hym one Fadir righte hande; and how His
dysciples turnede agayne into þe Cete, and ware in fastynge
and in prayere vntill þe commynge of þe Haly Gaste; and þare
ware togedire a hundreth and twentty in a house for to abyde
þe commynge of þe Haly Gaste, als oure Lorde commande þam
before. ¶ Before euensange sall þou thynke of Ihesu passion
and of His supere. Of þe passion sall þou thynke how Ioseph

II. *St. Edmund's Mirror. Meditations on the Last Supper.* 45

of Aramathy p*ur*chaste Ih*es*u body of Pilate, and how þey come *the Cross and the Lord's Supper before Evensong.*
to þe crosse þare He hang*e*, and þay brakke þe twa thee-banes
of þe twa thefes. And þare was a knyghte redye wi*th* a spere,
4 and p*er*chede þe syde of Ih*es*u, and smate Hym to þe herte; and
als sone come rynnande downe þe p*re*cyouse blode and wati*re*.
And þat was þe Rawnsone of þe whilke I be-fore spake—louede
be that Lorde!—And þa*n* Iosep*h* tuke Hym downe of þe crosse,
8 for-þi þat na bodye sulde duelle on þe crosse in so hye a daye
als was one þe morne. Of þe super*e* of Ih*es*u sa*ll* þou thynke, *The Supper of the Lord.*
how þat ty*m* He gafe His p*re*cyouse flesche and His blude in
lyknes of brede and of wyne þat we may See; and it es sothe-
12 fastely flesche and blude of Ih*es*u Criste, þat we may noghte See
wi*th* bodyli eghe*n*. Þe thirde thynge es gastely, þe grace þat
we rescheyue whe*n* we take þat flesche and þat blude. We se
þare lyknes of brede and of wyne, and it es noghte; bot we
16 trowe þat þare es sothefastly þe flesche and þe blude of Ih*es*u
Criste. And noghte forthi þe lyknes of flesche ne may we *Why Christ turned His flesh and blood into bread and wine.*
noghte see. And þare-fore, þare whare we sulde hafe vgglynes
als vn-ti*ll* oure body, for to ete flesche and drynke blude of ma*n*,
20 Oure Lorde Ih*es*u Criste t*ur*nede His flesche and His blude
in liknes of brede and of wyne, for to comforthe oure bodily
witte thurghe swylke fude als we ere wounte for to see, and
alswa for to helpe oure trouthe thurghe þat, þat we see
24 a thynge and trowes anoþ*er*. And þare-fore, dere frende, whe*n* *The disposition required in us.*
þou sa*ll* gaa for to reschaife þat swete flesche and þat blude
of Ih*es*u thi saueo*ur*, luke at þou haue verray contricyo*n*, and
repentance, and clensynge of thi sy*n* in thi herte; For þare þou
28 ressayfes in sacrament reghte als þou ressayfede Hy*m* in flesche
and blude—blescede be þat grace! ¶ Be-fore compl*y*n sa*ll* þou [† leaf 208.]
thynke how þat Iosep*h* and Nicodem*us* wande † Ih*es*u body XXVI.
in faire schetis, and enoynte it wi*th* p*re*cyouse oynementes, and *Before Compline the Agony and the Burial.*
32 laide it in a monumente of stane, and sett þaire seles apo*n*
þe stane, and knyghtes þat sulde it kepe. The toþ*er* thynge
þat þou sa*ll* thynke in þe same tyme es þis, how Ih*es*us, in þe
daye of super*e*, when He had souppede, He ȝode in-ti*ll* a gardy*n*
36 wi*th* His discyples, and felle downe in Orysou*n*, and byga*n* for

to swete one swilke manere þat þe droppis of blode droppede of His blyssede face vn-till þe erthe. Now hase þou matire and manere for to thynke of Goddis manhede. And eftirwarde salt þou wit how þou salt thynke one Hym in His heghe Godhede. ¶ To þat salt þou wit þat Godd temperd swa His knaweynge fra þe begynnynge of mankynde, þat He walde noghte all hally schewe Hym to man, ne all hally hele Hym fra man. For if He hade all hally schewede Hym to man, þan hadd trouthe noghte bene worthe and mysbileue had noghte bene þan ouercomen, For trouthe es of thynge þat may noghte be sene; þan þat at I see es noghte trouthe; and if He had all hallily helede fra man, þan had trouthe noghte bene helpede, and mysbileue hade bene excusede; and for-þi þan walde He in party schewe Hym, and in party hele Hym. Bot now may þou aske me, 'in how many maners He walde schewe Hym.' I say in twa maners, ane with-in, anoþer with-owtten. With-in He schewede Hym thurgh reuelacyon and thurgh resonn. With-owtten, thurgh halye writte and thurgh creaturs. Thurgh reuelacyon, when He schewede Hym till any folke thurgh inspiracion and thurghe myracle. By resonn, commes He till þe knawynge of man one þis manere:—Ilke a man may wele see in hym-selfe þat at he es, and þat at he hase bene, bot he may wele wit þat he hase noghte bene ay, and for þat he wate wele þat sum tym he be-gan for to be; þan was þaire sum tym when he was noghte. Bot when he was noghte, þan moghte he one na wyese make hym-selfe; and þis seghes man in his creature, For he sees ilke a day sum ga and sum com, For-þi, sen ilke thynges erre, and [1]þay erre noghte of[1] thaym selfe, þare-fore it behoues nede þat þare be ane to gyffe all thynges to be, þat es to saye of whaym alle thynges are; þare-fore it behoues of force þat He thurghe whaym alle thynges erre, be with-owtten begynnynge. For if He hade begynnyng, than it behoufede þat He had begynnyng of sum oþer; þan had He noghte bene þe first autour and þe fyrste begynnyng of all thyngez. Bot þare was na thynge before Hym, þan he come of na noþer, þan hade He neuer na begynnynge.

II. St. Edmund's Mirror. Why one God has Three Persons. 47

And þare-fore it behoufes one all maner of þe werlde, þat þare
be a thynge þat neuer hade begynnynge. And when reson of
man sese of force þat it may na noþer wysse be, þan he be-
4 gynnys for to trowe stabilly þat a thynge þat was with-owtten
begynnynge, þat es Awtour, and makere, and gouernere of all
thynges þat ere. And Hym calles men Godd by This skill,
For þis worde *Deus*, þat es to say, Godd, commes of a worde of
8 grewe þat es called *theos*, and þat es † als mekill for to say [† leaf 208 bk.]
als ane anely Godd. And þat betakyns þis worde Godd.

And, dere frend, þou awe to wit þat þare ne es bot a Godd, XXVIII.
and þou awe to wit þat na gude may faile to Godd. Bot for-þi And that there must be
12 þat swete thynge and gud thynge es comforthe of felaschepe, more than one Person in
þan may noghte Godd be with-owtten gudnes of felaschipe. the Godhead.
Than be-houede it nede þat þare ware many persones in Godd,
þe hegheste gudnes. And for-þi þat felyschepe may noghte be Fellowship necessitated
16 be-twyx faere þan twa, þare-fore be-houes it be þat in Godd two persons,
be at þe leste twa persones. And for-þi þat felyschipe es littill
worthe whare þare es nan Alyance ne lufe, For-thi it behoues
þat þe thirde person ware in Godd, þat ware the Alyance and
20 þe lufe be-twyx the twa. And for-þi þat anehede es gude, and
manyhede alswa, þare-fore it behouede nede þat anehede and and many-
manyhede bathe ware in Godd. And by þis skill commes man hood three in the One God.
to þe knaweynge of Godd, þat He es a Godd in Hymselfe, and
24 thre in persones. And þis ilke may man see in hym-selfe, For
he sese at þe begynnynge þat he hase in hym-selfe Powere, and
sythen eftir powere he hase wysdom. And sythen be-gane he
for to lufe þat wysdom; and þan begynnes he for to knawe
28 apertely þat þare es in þe saule Mighte, and of þat myghte
commes wysdom, and of thayme bathe comes lufe. And when
man sese þat it es one swylke manere in hym, Of þat awe hym
to wit þat one swylke man awe it to be in Godd þat es abouen
32 hym, þat es to say, þat in Godd es myghte, and of þat commes
his wysdome; and of powere and wysedom bathe comes lufe.
And for-þi þat of þe fyrste personne commes þe toþer, and owte
of thaym bathe comes þe thyrde, For-thi calles he þe firste The three
Persons of the
36 personne Godd þe Fadire, þe toþer Godd þe Sonne, þe thirde Trinity.

Godd' þe Haly Gaste. And for þat it wounte to be thus inmanges men, þat þe Fadir was mare Febill þan þe sonne, for
his elde, and þe sonne mare vnwyse þan þe Fadire for his
ȝouthe; and for þat a man sulde noghte wene þat it ware
swa of Godd, Therefore es powere appropirde to Godd' þe
Fadir, wysdom to Godd' þe Sonne. And for-þi þat þis worde
Gaste sownnes sumwhate into fellenes, For-þi es swetnes, lufe,
and gudenes appropirde to þe Haly Gaste. Oppon þis maner
commes man firste to þe knaweynge of his Godd, how He es
with-owtten be-gynnynge, and whi He es called Godd, ane in
substance and thre in persones, and whi þe firste persone es
callede Godd' þe Fadir, þe toþer, Godd' þe Sonne, þe thyrde,
Godd' þe Haly Gaste; and whi powere es appropirde to Godd'
þe Fadir, *and* wysdom to Godd' þe Sonne, and gudnes to
Godd' þe Haly Gaste. In swylke manere sall þou knawe þi
Godd.

XXIX.

The fyrste degre of contemplacion es, þat þe saule be ledde
agayne to þe selfe, and gedire it all with-in þe selfe. The
toþer degre es, þat man see whate he es, swa gedyrde to-gedire.
The thirde degre es, þat he lefte hym selfe abouen hym-selfe,
† and payne hym for to luke one his Godd' in his awen kynde.
Bot till selfe may he neuer mare comme, vntill he hafe lerede
to resayfe ilke a bodyly ymagynacyone erthely and gastely, þat
commes to his awen herte, owþer of herynge, or of tastynge,
or of sweloynge, or of any oþer bodily wite, to refuse it and to
defule it, þat it may see the selfe swylke as it es with-owtten
þe bodye. Thare-fore, dere Frende, take gud hede how þe
saule es wondirfull in þe selfe, and howe it es ane in þe kynde,
and noghte forthi ȝit it duse dyuerse thynges; For þe selfe, it
sese þat at þou sese with thyn eghne, heris with thyne eres,
Swelawes with thi mouthe, Smelles with þi nese, and al swa þat
at þou touches with all þi membris. ¶ Thynke ȝit Eftyrwarde,
howe þi saule es grete, þat all anely with a thoghte it may
comprehende heuen and erthe and all þat in þaym are, if
þay ware a hundreth falde grettere þan þay are or may be.

¶ When manes lyfe es grete and swa nobill þat na creature may

II. St. Edmund's Mirror. God's Mercy. Life of Love. 49

vndirstande it perfitly, Thane grete and nobiłł es he þat swa
nobiłł thynge made of noghte. He es abouen ałł thynge, and
with-in all thynge, and with-owtten all thynge, and be-nethe
4 ałł thynge. He is abouen ałł thynge, ałł thynge gouernande,
Be-nethe ałł thynge, berande ałł thynge, with-in ałł thynge,
Fulfillande ałł, with-owtten ałł thynge, abowte gangande ałł.

¶ Swylke manere of contemplacione Engendyrs in man Faste
8 trouthe and sekire deuocyone. ¶ Eftir þis sałł þou thynke howe *The bounty of God.*
þat he es large: and þat may þou see one many maners. See at
þe begynnynge howe þat he es large of erthely gude; how he
gyfes his gudes als wele to þe iłłe als to þe gude in alle thynges
12 þat þou sese in erthe. Sythen eftirward' see howe þat he es
large for to Forgyffe: For if a mane hym ane hade donne ałłs *His great mercy.*
mekiłł iłłe als ałłe þe men of þis werlde moghte doo, ȝitt sulde
he be mare redy be þe hundrethe parte for to Forgyffe hym þan
16 þat caytife sulde bee for to aske of hym forgyfenes.

¶ Nowe, my dere Frende, if þou lyfe eftir þis kennynge, þan XXX.
sałł þou lyfe honourabily,—and þat es þe fyrste parte of oure *This knowledge is the*
sermon þat I touchede at þe begynnynge,—and eftir þat sałł *way to live honourably,*
20 þou studye to lyffe lufely als to thyne euencrysten; and vntiłł *which was the first part*
þat sałł þou sette ałł hally þi myghte to lufe and for to be *of the Sermon.*
lufede. Thou sałł lufe ałł menne in Godd', þat es at say, anely *Next you must study to*
in gudnes, and noghte for þaire fairenes of bodye for to lufe, *live in love.*
24 ne for force, ne for na noþer bodily vertu. For þay þat lufes
in swylke manere, þay lufe noghte for Goddes sake; and for
to lufe man in Godd' es na noþer thynge bot for to lufe hym
for any thynge þat may noghte be lufede with-owtten Godd',
28 als for gudnes or for rightewysnes, or for sothefastenes. If we
do gude, þane hafe we na frende bot gude, ne nane Enemy bot
iłł; and þar-fore þase þat er gude sałł we lufe, for-thi þat þay
er gude, and þe ille sałł we lufe for-þi þat þay may be gude.
32 In þis manere lufe þou na thynge bot gudnes, sen þat þou lufes
ałł thynges for gudnes; and if þou wiłł be lufede, schewe thi
selfe lufely. Ife þou wiłł be lufely, resayfe these thre wordes
with-owtten forgetynge. Do þat at man biddis þe or praies *The way to shew true*
36 þe þat gude es; Take þat at man gyffes þe; and gruche noghte; *love.*

and þat at men will say þe, suffire it mekely, and wrethe the noghte. If þou lyfe þus lelely, þan lyfes thou lufely.

The way to live meekly.
Two ways of obtaining meekness;

Dere Syster and frende, Syen eftirwarde sall þou studye for to lyffe mekely; and to þis sall þou cwin wit þat þare are twa maners of mekenes. The tane commes of sothefastenes, and þe toþer commes of charite. †By þe firste may þou hafe knaweynge of thi selfe, For thou may noghte in na manere of þis worlde see þi selfe whate þou arte in sothefastenes, if þou be noghte mekyde. The toþer manere of meknes may þou hafe if thou thynke of þe meknes of Ihesu Criste, how þat he mekid hym þat neuer dyde syn; and swylke mekenes commes clenely of charyte.

[† leaf 209 bk.]
First, from knowing ourselves;
Second, from the example of Christ.

¶ Now, my dere syster and Frende, wate þou whate it es to lyffe honourabili, lufely, and mekely; and þat es to lyffe perfitly. Now oure swete Lorde Ihesu Criste gyffe vs grace, swa Godd for to honour, and oure euencristen for to lufe, and oure selfe for to meke, þat we may for oure honourynge be honourede, and for oure lufe be lufede, and for oure mekenes be lyftede vp in-to þe heghe blysse of heuen þat he boghte vs to, Ihesu with his swete blude and his preciouse passion. Amen!

These three things, To live honourably, lovingly, and meekly, make up the perfect life.

Explicit[1] speculum sancti Edmundi Cantuarensis Archiepiscopi. Dulce nomen Domini nostri Ihesu Christi: sit benedictum in secula seculorum! Amen!

[Follows, an English prose Treatise on the Lord's Prayer, 'Pater noster qui es in celis. In all the wordis þat are stabilled and sett to say in erthe,' &c.] Then comes, on leaf 211, the poem, 'Ihesu Criste, Saynte Marye sonne,' printed below, p. 79.

[1] MS. expliculum.

III. THE ABBEY OF THE HOLY GHOST.

[Robert Thornton's MS., Lincoln Cathedral Library, leaf 271.]

RELIGIO SANCTI SPIRITUS. RELIGIO MUNDA.

OFF the abbaye of saynte Spirite, that es in a place that [leaf 271.]
es callede conscyence.

A, dere brethir and systirs! I see þat many walde be in *Because many are* religyon, bot þay may noghte, owthir for pouerte, or for drede *hindered from actually tak-* of thaire kyn, or for band of Maryage; and for-thi I make *ing religious vows, he will*
4 here a buke of þe religeon of þe herte, þat es, of þe abbaye *make a book of the religion* of the Holy Goste, that all tho þat ne may noghte be bodyly *of the heart.* in religyon, þat þay may be gostely. A, Ihesu, Mercy! whare may þis abbay beste be funded, and þis religione? Now certis *The Abbey of the Holy*
8 nowhare so wele als in a place þat es called 'conscyence'; and *Ghost Consciencia.* who so will be besy to funde þis holy religion, and þat may *founded in a place called* ilke gud crystyn man and woman do, þat will he besy þer- *Conscience.* abowte. And at þe begynnynge it es by-houely þat þe place
12 of thi conscience be clensed clene of syn; to þe whilke clensynge þe Haly Goste sall sende two maydyns þat ere conande: the *The maidens that cleanse* one es callede 'rightwysnes,' and þe toþer is called 'luffe of *the place, Righteous-* clennes.' Thiese two sall cast fro þe conscience and fro þe *ness and Purity.*
16 herte, all maner of fylthe of foule thoghtes and desyris. When þe place of þe conscience es wele clensed, than sall þe grownde be mad lange and depe; and thies two maydenes sall be made, þe one es callede 'Mekenes,' þat sall make þe grownde depe *Meekness and Poverty pre-*
20 thorowe lowlynes of hir selfe, the toþer es callede 'Pouerte,' *pare the ground.* þat makis it large & wyde abowne, þat castis ouer ylke a halfe þe erthe owte, þat es to say, alle erthely lustes & worldely thoghtes ferre fro þe herte, þat, if þay hase erthely gudis, with
24 luffe þay for-gete þaym for þe tym, & castis no lufe to þam, nor hase noghte, ne settis noghte for þat tyme þaire hertes no thynge one þam. And thies ere called 'pure in spyrite,' of wham God spekes in þe gospelle, & sayse þat 'thaires es þe

kyngdom of heuen, be thies wordes *Beati pauperes spiritu,* [Matt. v. 3.]
quoniam ipsorum est regnum*' *cœlorum.* Blyssed es þan þat [* MS. rignum.]
religyon þat es funndide in pouerte and in meknes. This es
agaynes many religyous þat are couetous and prowde. 4

This abbaye also sall be sett on a gud reuer, and þat sall   The Abbey built on a good river, The River of Tears.
be þe reuer of teres. For swylke abbayes þat ere sett one
swylke gude ryuers, þay are wele at ese, and þe more dylecyous
duellyng es þer. †One swylke a reuer was Mary Mawdelayne 8   [† leaf 271 bk.]
fowndide, For-thy grace and rechesse come all to hir will, and
for-thi sayde Dauid thus, *Fluminis impetus letificat ciuitatem,*   [Ps. xlv. 5.]
þat es to saye, 'the gude reuer mase þe Cete lykande,' for it es
clene sekyr, & ryche of all gude marchandyse. And so þe 12
reuer of teris clenses Goddis cete, þat es, mannes saule, þat
es Goddes cete. And also þe holy man sayse of fylthe of
synn, þat it brynges owte þe reches of vertus and of alle gude
thewes. And when þis grownde es made, þan sall come 16
a damaselle, Bowsomnes, on þe tone halfe, and damaselle
Miserecorde one þe toþer halfe, for to rayse þe walles one   Obediencia. Misericordia. The walls raised by Obedience and Mercy.
heghte, and to make þam stalworthe, with a fre hert largely
gyfande to þe pure, & to þam þat myster hase. For when we 20
do any gud werkes of charite thorow þe grace of Gode, als
ofte sythis als we þam do in þe lufe and þe louynge of God, and
in gud Entent, als many gud stonys we laye one owre howssynge
in þe blysse of heuen, festenande togedir with þe lufe of Gode 24
and oure euen-crysten. We rede þat Salomon made his   Salomon.
howssynge of gret precyouse stones. Thiese precyous stones
are almos-dedis and werkes of mercy, & holy werkes þat sall
be bownden to-gedir with qwyke lyme of lufe & stedfaste 28   The Love of God and right Faith are the cement.
by-leue. And for-thi sayse Dauid, *Omnia opera eius in fide,*
þat es to saye, 'alle his werkes be done in stedfaste by-leue.'   Dauid. [Ps. xxxii. 4.]
And als a walle maye not laste with-owtten syment, or more,
also no werkes þat we wyrke, are noghte worthe to God, nor 32
spedfull till oure sawles, bot þay be done in the lufe of God
and in trewe by-leue. For alle þat þe synfull dose, alle es loste.   Paciencia. Fortitudo.
Sythen Dameselle Sufferance and damesell Forte sall rayse   Patience and Strength shall raise the pillars,
þe pelars, & vndirsett þam so strangly, þat no wynde of wordes, 36

III. Abbey of the Holy Ghost. Its Builders, Officers, &c.

angre of stryffe, fleschely nor gastely, sowre ne swete, caste þaim downe. A, dere brethir and systers, ȝitt by-houys þe cloystyre be made one foure corners; and it es callede 'cloyster' *Claustrum.*
4 for it closys and steskys, and warely sall be lokkede. My dere *There must be a Cloister to keep from* breþir and systyrs, wylke of ȝow as will halde this gastely *evil.* religyon, & be in ryste of sawle & in swetnes of hert, halde þe with-in þe cloyster, and so sparre þou þe ȝates, and so
8 warely kepe þou þe wardes of þi cloyster, þat no noþer fandyngez nor euylle styrrynges hafe in-gate in the, & make þat thy Sylence, † and for to [   ] the, or styrre the to synn [1], [†leaf 272.] steke thyn eghne fro fowle syghtes, thyn heres fro foule
12 herynges, thy Mouthe fro foule speche, and thyn herte fra foule thoghtes. Scrifte sall [make] thi chapitir, Predicacion *Confessio. Predicacionne.* sall make thi fratour, Oracion sall make thi chapelle, Con- *Oracio.* templacione sall make thi dortoure, þat sall be raysede one *Shrift shall make the Chapter-*
16 heghte with heghe ȝernynge, and with lufe qwykkynynge to *house; Preaching* Gode, and þat sall be owte ofe worldly noyse and of worldly *the Fratour; Prayer the* angyrse and besynes, als fere furthe als þou may for þe tym *Chapel; Con- templation* thorow grace for þe tym of prayere. Contemplacion es a *the Dormi- tory.*
20 deuote rysynge of herte with byrnynge lufe to God to do wele, *Contem- placion.* and in his delites Ioyes his saule, and somdele ressayues of that swetnes þat Goddis chosen childir sall hafe in heuen. Rewfulnes sall make the fermorye, Deuocion sall make þe *Rewfulnes. Deuocion.*
24 celere, Meditacion sall make the gernere. *Meditacion.*

And when all þe howses bene made, þan be-houes þe Holy *Sadness the Infirmary;* Gaste Ordeyne þe couent of grace & of vertu. And þan sall þe *Devotion the Cellar; Medi- tation the* Holy Gaste þat þis religyone es of, bee warden and visiture, *Store-house.*
28 the whilke God þe Fadir funded thorow his powere. For þus *The Holy Ghost the Warden and* saise Dauide, *Fundauit eam altissimus,* and this es to saye, 'the *Visitor.* heghe Gode þe Fadyr Fundide this relegyone.' The Son thurgh his wysedom þan ordayned it, als Sayne Paule witnes *Paulus.*
32 it, *Que adeo ordinata sunt,* þat es at saye, 'alle þat es of God the Sone, it rewlis & ordaynes.' The Holy Goste ȝemys it and vesettes it; and þat saye [we] in holy kyrke when we saye þis,

---

[1] There is some confusion in this sentence from the omission of one or more words.

III. *Abbey of the Holy Ghost. Officers: Abbess Charity, &c.*

Veni Creator Spiritus, with *Qui paraclitus diceris*, þat es for to saye, 'come, þou God þe Haly Gaste, and thyne þou vesete, and fulfill þam with grace.' And than the gude lady Charite, als scho þat es most worthy by-fore alle oþer, sall be abbas 4 of this sely abbaye. And also, als þay þat are in relegyone sall do no thynge, ne saye thynge, ne gange in-to no stede, ne take no gyfte, with-owtten leue of þe abbasse. Also gastely sall none of swylke thyngys be done with-owtten leue of charite, 8 For thus commandes Sayne Paule, *Omnia vestra in caritate fiant*, þat es, 'what-so ȝe do, or saye, or thynke with herte, alle ȝe mon do in charite.' A, dere breþir and systirs, whate here es harde comandement! Bot it es noghte full ill to oure sawles 12 þat oure thoghtes & oure wordes & oure werkes be onely done for lufe. Wayleawaye! if I durste saye! for many are in religione, bot to fewe religious, þat þay ne done þe comandment of saynte Paule, or þe concelle of þe †gud lady Charite, þat 16 es abbesse of this cely relegyon. And for-thi þay lose mekill tym, and losses þaire mede, and ekes thaire payne gretly, bot if þay amende þam, whare-fore, leue breþir and systirs, bese euer-more wakire and warre; and in all ȝoure werkes, thynke 20 depely þat whate-so ȝee doo, be it done in þe lufe of Gode, and for þe lufe of þe lady Wysdome þat sall be prioresse; for scho es worthi, *Nam, prior omnium creata est sapiencia*, þat es, 'al-þir-firste es Wysedome made'; and thurgh þe lare of hir, 24 and þe concele of þis prioresse, sall we do alle þat we do; and this sayse Dauid, *Omnia in sapiencia fecisti*, þat es at saye, 'alle þat þou hase made, þou hase made wysely.' The gud lady Meknes þat aye Elyke makis hir selfe lowly and vndir 28 alle oþer, sall be supprioresse: hir sall ȝe honoure and wirchipe with bouxomnes. A Ihesu! blyssede þat abbaye, and cely es þat religyone, þat hase so haly ane abbas as Charyte, a prioresse as Wysedome, a supprioresse as Mekenes. A, dere breþir and 32 systirs, blyssede and Cely are þay, þat es to say, those saules are cely þat haldis þe comandment of þe abbas lady Charite, and þe techynge of þe priores, lady Wysdome, and the concele of þe suppriorese, lady mekenes; For who-so es bouxome to 36

III. *Abbey of the Holy Ghost. Officers: Discretion, Prayer.*

thir thre ladyse, and þaire lyffe rewlis aftir þaire techynge, *Thou who obey Charity,*
the Fadir, the Sone, the Holy Goste, þam sall comfurthe with *Wisdom, and Meekness*
many gostely Ioyes, and þam helpe and socoure in alle fandinges, *win God's comforting,*
4 in angirs, þat þay ne be noghte ouercomen; þam thare drede
no wrenkis ne no wylis of the fende, for why God es with
þam, and standis aye by þam als a trewe kepere & a strange.
And for-þi says Dauid thus, *Dominus protector vite mee, a quo* [Ps. xxvi. 1.]
8 *trepidabo?* als if he sayd, 'God es my champyone staleworthe
and trewe, þat for me, þat es so wayke and so vnmyghtfull,
agaynes myn Enemyse hase vndirtane for to fyghte: whame
thare me þan drede? now trewly, righte none.' We rede in
12 a buke of Danyele þat a myghtfull was þat men callede
Nabogodhonosore, þat sett in Rome thre men þat solde do
& ordayne and stabyll, als baylyes, alle þe rewme, so þat þe
kynge herde no noyse, ne no playnte, bot þat he myghte be in
16 pese, & in Ioye, & in ryste in his rewme. And righte so þe
rewme of þe sawle þat thiese thre baylyes are In, and þe
religione þat thies thre prelates are In, þat es, Charite, Wyse-
dome and Mekenes, thare es pese, ryste, and lykynge in saule, *and peace, rest, and*
20 and comforthe in lyfe. *bliss.*

Damsele Discrecyone, þat es witty and be full ware, sall be *Discretion the Treasurer.*
tresorere; scho sall hafe in hir kepynge alle, † and ȝernely [† leaf 273.]
luke þat all go wele. Orysone salle be chaunterese, þat with *Orysone.*
Oryson the
24 hertly prayers sall trauele daye & nyghte. And whate Orysone *Chauntress.*
es, þe haly man sayse, *Oracio est Deo sacrificium, angelis
solacium, diabolo tormentum,* þat es to saye, 'Orysone es
a louely sacrafice to God, Solase and lykynge to Angells, and
28 turment to þe fende.' It witnes in the lyfe of Saynte Barthilmewe, þat it es turment to þe fende; for þe fende cryede to
hym and sayde *Bartholomee! incendunt me oraciones tue,* þat es *Diabolus.*
Bartholo-
to saye, 'Bertilmew, thi prayers byrnys me.' And þat es *meus.*
32 lykynge to angels, Saynte Bartilmew wytnes it, and sayse,
'when we praye with deuocyone of hert, the Angels standis *Angels carry*
our prayers
byfore, daunsesande & prayeande, and beris oure prayers vp, *up to God.*
and a present of þam to þe Fadir of heuen. Þe whilke prayers
36 oure Lorde commandes to wryte in þe buke of lyfe, þat es,

sacrafyce to God: this are of þam þat hym moste payes; and
for-thi he askes vs it þer he sayse thus, *Sacrificium laudis*
[Ps. xlix. 43.] *honorificabis me*, þat es to saye, 'ȝe salle wyrchipe with
Iubilacio. sacrifice of louynge.' *Iubilacio* hir felowe sall helpe; and,
Jubilation the helper of the Chauntress. what Iubilacion es, a seynt it telles, and sayse þat Iubylacion
es a grete Ioye þat es consayuede in teris, thorow brynnande
luffe of spirite, þat may noghte be in all schewede, no in alle
hyde, als it fallis somtyme of tho þat God hertly lufes: þere-
eft*ir* þat þay hafe bene in p*r*ayere and in orysone, þay ere so
lyghte & so lykande in God þat, whare-so þay go, þer hertes
synges murnynge songes of lufe-longynge to þaire lefe, þat þay
ȝerne w*ith* armys of lufe semlyly to falde, and w*ith* gastely
mo*ur*ny[n]ge of his gudnes swetly to kysse, and ȝit vmwhile so
depely, þat wordis þam wanttis, for luf-longynge so ferforthe
rauesches thorow hertis, þat somtym þay ne wote noghte whate
Deuocion. þay do. Deuocione es celeresse, þat kepis þe wynnes, bothe þe
Devotion the Cellaress. white and þe rede, w*ith* depe vmbythynkynge of þe gudnes
of God, & of þe paynnes & of þe anguyse þat he tholede, and
of the Ioyes & þe delytes of paradyse, þat he hase ordayned
Penance. to his chosen. Penance sall be kychynnere, þat w*ith* grete
Penance the Cook. besynes trayuells daye & nyghte for to plese alle, and ofte
swetis w*ith* bitt*er* teris for angyre of hir synnes. Scho makes
gud metis, þat es, many bitt*er* sorowes alle for hir gyltez. And
[† leaf 273 bk.] †theys metis fedis þe saule, bot scho sparis hir-selfe thorow
abstynence, and etys bot littill; For, do scho neu*er* so mekill ne
so mony-folde of gude werkes, ay semys scho hir-selfe vnworthy
Atemper-ance. and synfull. Atemp*er*ance seruede in the frato*ur* þat scho to
Temperance the Waiter. ylkone so lukes þat mesure be ou*er* alle, þat none ou*er* mekill
Sobyrnes. nere ou*er* lyttill ete ne drynke. Sobirnes redis at þe borde
Soberness the Reader. the lyues of the haly Fadirs, and synges and rehercees whate
lyfe þat þay lede for to take gud Ensampille to do als þay dyd,
Pete. and þere thorowe slyke mede to wyn als þay now hafe. Pete
Pity the Answerer. es spensere, þat dose seruesse to gud, all þat scho maye. And
Mercy. Mercy hir syst*er* sall be ambynowre, þat gyffes to alle, and
Mercy the Almoner. noghte kane kepe to hir-selfe. The lady Drede es portere,
Drede. Dread the Porteress. þat kepis besyly þe cloyst*er* of þe herte, & of þe co*n*science

III. *Abbey of the Holy Ghost. Its Officers: Reason, &c.*

þat chases owte alle vnthewes, and calles In alle gud vertus,
& so speres þe ȝatis of þe cloyster & þe wyndows, þat none
evylle hafe none Ingate to þe herte, thorowe þe ȝatis of þe
4 mouthe, ne thorowe þe wyndows of þe eghne, nere of þe eris.
Honeste es Maystresse of þe nouyce, and teches þam alle curtasye, *Honeste Magister Nouiciarum.* Honesty the Mistress of the Novices.
how þay sall speke and gange, and sytt and stande, and how
þay sall bere þam with-owtten and with-in; howe to God,
8 how to man, so þat alle þat þam sese, of þam may take
ensampill of alle gudnes, and alle gude thewes. Dameselle
Curtasye sall be hostelere; & þat þay comande & byddes, þat *Curtasye.* Courtesy and
scho sall þam resafe hendely, so þat ylke one may speke of
12 hir. And for-thi þat nowþer sall be by þam one emange the
gestes,—For it myghte falle þat damselle Curtasye solde be oure
balde a[nd] ouer hardy,—for-thi sall scho hafe a felawe Damesele,
Symplese; for þay two alyede to-gedir thorowe felawchipe, are *Simplicity the receivers of*
16 sekyre and semande, for þe tone with-owtten þe toþer vmwhile *the guests. Why two*
es littill worthe. For ouer-grete symplesse may make of þe *receivers are needed.*
symple a sott, or ouer nyce, and ouer-grete curtasye may be
somewhile oþer to lyghte chere or to glade, or ouer-balde, for
20 to paye þe gestes; Bot fayre and wele, & with-owtten fandynge
of blame, may þay do þaire Offece both to-gedir.

Damesele Resone sall be puruerere, For scho sall ordayne *Resone.*
with-in & with owttyn so skilfully, þat þere ne be no defaute. *Reason the Purveyor.*
24 Damesele Lewte sall be fermoresse, þat sall trauelle abowte, *Service shall attend to the*
& besely serue þe seke. And for-þi sen þat in þe fermory of *hospital and nurse the*
this religyon are moo seke þam hole, mo febyll þan wighte, *sick.*
and es ouer-grete trauelle to serue þam alle hyr one, †For-thi [†leaf 274.]
28 sall scho hafe a felawe, Damesele Largesse, þat sall see full *Largitas.*
wele to ylkone after þat þam nedis. Damesele Conande and *Largess shall help her.*
Wysse, þat es callede Meditacyone, or Poleschesy, es garnere: *Poleschey. Meditation*
scho sall gedyre and sembyll gude whete and oþer gud cornnes *the store-keeper,*
32 to-gedir, and þat fully, with grete plente, thorowe þe whilke
alle þe gud ladyse of þe howse may hafe þaire sustenance.
Meditacion es in gud thoghtes of God, & of his werkes, and *Meditacion.*
of his wordes, and of his creaturs, and of his paynnens þat *In thoughts of God.*
36 he tholede, and of his grete lufe þat he had and hase to þam

III. *Abbey of the Holy Ghost. Its Officers: Meditation.*

<small>David had a like granary.</small> for whaym he tholede. This garnere had þe gud kyng Dauid; For-þi was he ay riche & in plente, and for-þi he sayse in þe
<small>[Ps. lxxi. 13.]</small> psaltyre, *In omnibus operibus tuis Meditabar die ac nocte*, þat es to saye, 'Lorde! in thi lawe I thynke nyghte and daye.' This es begynnynge of all perfeccion, than when man settis and stabylls his herte in depe thynkynge on God & on his <small>A good thought is better than words of prayer.</small> werkes. For ofte es better a gud thoghte in haly meditacyon þan Many wordes sayd in prayere, For þe holy thoghtes in meditacion cryes in Goddes eris. Ofte it falles þat þe herte es so ouer-tane and so raueschede in holy meditacyon, þat it wote noghte what it dose, heris, nor sayse, or seys; so depely es þe herte festenede in God and in his werkes, þat wordis hym wanttis; and þe stillere þat he es in slyke Meditacion, the luddere he cryes in Goddes eris; and þer-fore sayd Dauid thus,
<small>[Ps. xxxi. 3.]</small> *Quoniam tacui dum clamarem tota die*, as if he sayd, 'Lorde! lo, here, the whills myn herte was in depe thoghtes in the and of thi werkes, it cryed one the in holy Medytacyons, and was stylle, as beynge domme.' And þer sayse þe glose, 'the grete cryes þat we crye to God þan, are oure grete desyres and oure grete ʒernynges.' And this sayse Saynte Denyse, þat sayse, 'When þe herte es lyfte and raueschede to þe lufe of God with gelouse ʒernynges, he ne may sownde with worde þat þe herte <small>Meditation is the Granary that keeps the wheat of Christ's body.</small> thynkis.' This holy Meditacione, þat es, þe gernare þat kepis ʒerely þe whete þat es rede with-owte and white with-in, þat hase þe syde clouen, of þe whilke men mase gud brede, þat es called Ihesu Criste, þat with-owtten was rede of his awen blode, and whitte with-in thorow his awen mekenes and <small>[† leaf 274 bk.]</small> clennes of lyfe, and hade † his syde clouen with a spere,—this <small>Sacramentum Altaris. Meditacion. Deuocion.</small> es þe brede þat we ressayue and etis in þe Sacrament of þe altyr. And wele þou weite þat the gerner sall be abown þe Selare, also sall be Meditacion before deuocion; and for-thi <small>Devotion the Cellarer.</small> meditacion sall be gernare, Deuocion Celerrere, and Pete pene- <small>Pietas. Pity the Penitancer, or Pittancer.</small> tancere[1]. Of thiese thre sayse þe profete Dauide[2] *A Fructu frumenti vini, et olei sui, multiplicati sunt*, þat es at saye, 'Of

---

[1] Sic in MS.; but ?*pittancere*, i. e. the officer who served out the rations. The Prioress had charge of the discipline. [2] Ps. iv. 8.

III. *Abbey of the Holy Ghost. Its Wheat, Wine, & Oil.*

the fruyte of þe whete and wyne and oyle, þay ere fulfillede.'
In þe alde lawe, in many stedis, Gode takis to his chosenn thiese
thre. 'Serue me,' he sayse, 'wele, & I saƚƚ gyffe ȝowe plente *The wheat, wine, and oil*
4 of whete and wyne & oyle.' Plente of whete es, hertly to *of the Abbey.*
thynke one þe croyce, and euer haffe þe passyonn of Ihesu Crist *The wheat is Meditation.*
hertly in mynde. This es Meditacionn. Plente of wyne, þat *The wine, Devotion.*
es þe weƚƚe of teres; wele for to wepe, this es Deuocionn. *The oil is Delight in God.*
8 Plente of oyle, þat es, for to hafe delyte and sauoyre in God;
and this es comforthe, for þe oyle gyffes odoure to metis, and
lyghtes in þe kyrke, and byrnys in þe lampe. Also whenn
Goddis seruandes hase depely thoghte with schire herte on
12 Gode, & on his werkes, with lufe-longynge to þamm, þann hase
God pete of þamm, and sendis þam petance of comforthe and of
gastely Ioye; and this gyffes hym at þe begynnnyng Meditacionn,
and þis es þe whete þat God hyghttes vs, and deuocyone þat
16 men consayues in medytacyonn. Than sendis God sone after
þe wyne, þat es, plente of teris; and after, þe wyne of swete *Virtus Vini.*
teris; than sendys he þe oyle of consolacionn, þat gyffes þam *The wine is Tears; the oil, Consola-*
Sauour, & lyghtnes his knaweliggynge, and schewes to þam of *tion.*
20 his heuenly priuatyse, þat es hide fro þamm þat folowes fleschely
desyris, and gyffes þamm selfe aƚƚe to þe wysedome of þe worlde
and his fantasyse, and so enflawmes þam with þe blysse of his
lufe þat þay taste somedelle, & fele how swete he es, how gud
24 he es, how luffande he es—bot noghte aƚƚe fully. I wote wele
þat none may fele it fully, bot if his herte sulde bryste for
lykynge of Ioye. Sayne Austyne telles of a preste þat, whenn *Saint Austin's story of a*
he herde any thynge of God þat lykynge ware Inn, he wold be *priest.*
28 so raueschede in Ioye þat he walde faƚƚ downe, and lygge als
he ware dede. And also in þat tyme, if men layde byrnande
fyre to his flesche nakide, he felid † it no more þan dose a dede [† leaf 275.]
corse. Sayne Bernarde spekes of þe wordis of Iob, þer he *Barnardus.*
32 sayse *Abscondit lucem in manibus*, þat es at say, 'God hase *Saint Bernard on the light of God.*
lyghte hyde in his handis.' Þou wote wele, he þat hase a
candiƚƚ lyghte by-twene his handis, he may hyde it & schewe
it at his owenn wiƚƚ. So dose oure Lorde to his chosenn.
36 Whenn he wiƚƚ, he opynis his handes, and lyghtenes þam with

III. Abbey of the Holy Ghost. The Clock of the Abbey.

heuenly gladnes; and when he witt, he closis his handis, and withdrawes þe lykynge & þe comforthe fro þam. He witte noghte þat þay fele it fully aye, Bot here he gyffes þam as for to taste & sauour somedele how swete he es, how gud he es: als Dauid sayse, *Gustate & videte quam suauis est Dominus*, als if God sayd to vs, 'be þis comforthe and this lykynge þat þou þis schorte tym hase of me, þou may taste & fele how swete, how gude I ame to my chosyn in my blysse, in þe werlde with-owtten ende'; and þus he dose, for to drawe vs fro worldly besynes, and þe lykynge þer-of, and for to enflawme oure hertes with lufe-ȝernynges, For to wyn and to hafe þe lykynge of þat Ioye, atte at þe futt in body and saule, with hym for to be euer more with-owtten ende.

Markers: God gives His chosen a taste of His sweetness here. [Ps. xxxiii. 9.]

A dameselle wyse & wele taghte, þat men calles Gelosye, þat es ay wakyre and besy euerylyke wele for to do, satt kepe þe orloge, and satt wakkyn þe oþer ladyse, & make þam arely to ryse, and go þe wyllylyere to þaire seruysse. Þer es orloges in towne þat wakyns men to ryse to bodily trauayle, & þat es þe seke; and þer es orloges in þe cete þat wakynnes þe marchauntes to wende a-bowte þaire marchandyce, þat es þe wynde þat blawes daye. And þer es orloges in religion of contemplacion. And this es of this holy relegyon þat es fundede of þe Haly Gaste, and þis es Ielosy; and this es sauoyre of perfeccion. & ofte it falles in relegion, be-fore þat þe Orloge falles or any belles rynges, Goddes gostely seruandes are lange wakenede before, and hase wepede by-fore God, and hase waschen þam with þaire teris, and þaire spyrit hase † vesete with deuote prayers and gastely comforthe. And why rose þay so arely & so tymly? Witterly for þe orloge of lufe; and damesele Ielosye had wakened þam be-fore þe tyme þat þe handmayde orloge fette. A, dere breþir and syster! sely ar tho sawles þat þe lufe of God, and longyng titt hym, wakyns, and slomers noghte, no slepis noghte, in þe slowthe of fleschly lustes. For-thi he sayse in Canticis, *Ecce dormio, et cor meum vigilat*,[1] þat es at saye, 'when I slepe bodily, my flesche for

Markers: Jealousy shall be watcher and time-keeper. There are clocks in religion. Before they strike, folk often rise to weep. [† leaf 275 bk.] and pray, for damsel Jealousy woke them. [Cant. v. 2.]

---
[1] MS. *vigelat*.

III. *Abbey of the Holy Ghost. Wicked Nuns: Envy, &c.*

to ese & ryste, my herte es ay wakyre in gelosy and in lufe-ȝernynge to Gode.' That saule þat þus wakes to God, me thynke hole conscyence þat werldly meñ thynke, and þat es
4 this, *Jeo ay le quer a leche, rauaylé par amours,* þat es at saye, 'Myñ herte es styrte fro me, wakened with lufe.' Whate es this þat mase þe herte fro þe flesche to wake, and for þat es it, as it were, fremde to hym? Wittirly Ieloussye with lufe, teres,
8 & murnynge, with lufe-longynge consaynede in deuote vprysynge of herte.

When this Abbaye was alle wele ordaynede, and Goddes will seruede in ryste, & in lykynge, & in pese of saule, than come
12 a tyrante of þe lande thorowe his powere, and did in this holy Abbaye Foure doghtyrs þat he hade þat were lothely & of euyll maners, þat þe fende was fadyr of thiese doghtyrs. Þe firste þer-of, þis foule barne-tyme, highte Envye; the toþer
16 highte Pride; the thirde highte Gruchynge; the ferthe highte False Demynge of oþer. Thiese foure doghetirs þan hase þe tyraunt, þe deueil of helle, for euyll will & malese, done in this holy Abbaye; and þay, with þaire foule vnclennes, þe couent hase
20 greuede and harmede, so þat þay no riste ne no pete may hafe, nyghte nor daye, nor lykynge in saule. And when þe gud lady Charite saw this (þat was Abbas), and the lady Wysedome (þat was prioresse), and þe lady Mekenes, supprioresse, and þe toþer
24 gude ladyse of this holy Abbaye, that the holy Abbaye was in poynte for to worthe to noghte thorowe þe wykkydnes † of [† leaf 276.] thir foure, Than range [þay] þe chapetour belle, and gedirde þam alle to-gedir, and asked concele whate was beste to do. And
28 than lady Dyscrecyoñ þam concelde þat þay solde alle falle in prayere to þe Holy Goste, þat of this Abbay es vesetour, þat he haste hym for to come, as þay grete myster hade, þare for to helpe and vesete with his grace. And þay all, at hire
32 consaile, with grete deuocyoñ of herte vnto hym, sange alle with a swete steueñ, *Veni, creator spiritus!* And also sone þe Holy Goste come at þaire desyrynge, and þam comforthede with his grace, and chasede owte þe fowle wyghtes,
36 þose lothely fendis doghetirs, and clenesede þe Abbaye of all

Quatuor filias diaboli.
Four evil damsels introduced into the Abbey— Envy, Pride, Grumbling, Evil-thinking.

The mischief they did.

Caritas. Sapiencia. Humilitas.

Discrecioñ.
The counsel of Lady Discretion, to pray to the Holy Ghost.

He, as Visitor of the Abbey expels the evil damsels.

<small>Let Charity, Wisdom, and Meekness dwell in your hearts.</small> þe fylthe, and ordayned it, and restorede better þaɴ it was by-fore. Now I pray ȝow all in charite of God, þat all þa þat of this relegioɴ redis or heris, þat þay be bouxome wíth all þaire myghte, and suffire þat þe gud ladys be-fore namede do 4 þaire offece ilke daye gastely wíth-in þaire hertes. And luke ylkone wysely þat he ne do no trispase agayne þe rewle ne þe obedyence of þis relegioɴ, and of þase lufe-frayners. And if <small>If you are in sin, pray for God's help, and you shall be delivered.</small> thorow vnhape falle þat any of thiese foure fendis doghetirs 8 seke one any wyse any Ingate for to hafe wíth-in ȝoure hertes for to duelle, or Ingate hase wonne, and wíth ȝow duellis, do so, after þe concelle of þe lady Discrescioɴ, and gyffe ȝow to deuocioɴ wíth hertly prayers, in hope of Goddes helpe and of his socoure, 12 and ȝe sall be delyuerde thurgh þe mercy of oure Lord Ihesu Criste there. Blyssede mot he be wíth-owtteɴ ende! Ameɴ!

Explicit Relegio Sancti Spiritus. Ameɴ.

[Follows, on leaf 276, bk. 277, the Poem 'The begynnyng as of thee.']

IV. WILLIAM OF NASSINGTON'S POEM ON THE TRINITY AND UNITY, THE PASSION OF CHRIST, &c.

[430 *lines in 4-measure couplets, each couplet written as one line.*]

Incipit Tractatus Will*e*lmi Nassyngtoñ, quonda*m* aduocati [leaf 189.]
Iur*is* Ebor*aci*, de Trinitate & Vnitate, *cum* declarac*ione* ope*r*um
Dei, & de passione *Do*m*i*ni no*st*ri Ihe*s*u *Christ*i, &c.

<table>
<tr><td>

A lord' God of myghte*s* maste,
   Fade*r*, and Soñ, and Haly Gaste.
   Fader, for þou ert almyghtty,
Soñ, for þou ert all wytty,
Haly Gaste, for thow all wyll
That gude is, and na thynge yll,
A God' and ane Lord' yn threhed',
And' thre persons yn anehede,
Thus was thow aye, and eue*r* sall be,
Thre yn ane, and' ane yn thre.
And begynnynge and' end of all thatt is,
And' þat eue*r* was, bathe mare & lesse;
Begynnynge, wi*th*-outteñ begynnynge,
And' ende, wi*th*-outeñ endynge;
Thatt, be-for any thynge wer wroghtt,
Or any begynnynge was, or oghtt,
And' befor all tymes, God' was thow,
& Allmygtty & wysse, as þou ert now;
Thy myght & thy witt, of thy selfe whas tane,
For neu*er* God was bo[t] þou ane.
And alls þou was Gode ay suthefaste,
Swa sall þi Godhede eu*er*-mare laste;

</td><td>

Thanksgiving to the adorable Trinity.

4

8
The nature of God.

12
He is without beginning or end.

16

[lf. 189 bk.]
20

God is eternal.

</td></tr>
</table>

IV. William of Nassington's Poem.

    And alls þou began all þat euer was,
    Swa sall þou Ende all þat sall passe.   24
Blessed be He!   Louede and blyssede ay mote þou be,
    And with all my herte I thankë the,
    Of all þat þou has done and wroghte,
    Fra þe firste tym̄ þat þou began oghte   28
    For me and for all man-kynde.
    Whare-fore vs aghte ay haue þe in mynde,
We should love Him.   And loue þe for [all] þou has done to mane,
    Als I here, thurgh þi grace, reherse cane.   32
By God all things were made.   Fyrste, heuen & erth, for man þou made,
    & all þis werlde here, wyd & brade,
    And al thyng þat es þer-In,
    For with-owtten the es noghte bot synn,   36
    The wilke was neuer thurgh the wroghte;
    Þer-for in haly writt es synn called noghte.
Heaven,   Heuen þou made, whare þou duelles,
    For oure Endles wōnny[n]ge with angells;   40
the world.   And þe werlde, owre suget here to be,
    To serue vs, þat we þare-In serue þe.
    The firmament þou made mouande,
    To noresche all thyng þare-vndire lyfande,   44
Sun, moon, and stars, &c.   And the sonne, to schede þe day fra þe nyght,
    And þe mone & þe sternes to tak þaire lyghte
    Of þe sonne for to schyne one nyghte clere,
    In takynyng þat we sall reschaife here   48
    The lighte of grace, þat gastely gifte es,
    Of þe, þat es sonne of ryghtwisnes.
    The mone lyghte, thow made to waxe and wane,
    Alls semes þat Ensample þer-by es tane,   52
    Of owre lyfe, þat passes here sonne,
    & waxes & wanes als lyghte of þe Monne.
    The sternës þou made, on þe sky standande,
planets, all as examples to us.   & the planettes, in þeire course passande,   56
    For Ensaumple til vs, to knawë & se
    How we sulde liffe here in ilke a degre.

The foure Elementës, þou mad sere,
To sustayne oure bodyly kynde here ;   60
And all oþer creatoures, als was thi will,
In sere kyndes þou made for certayn skyll ;
Of wilke, som are noyeand till vs .kyndly,
And som are profytable and Esye ;   64
And all are they for owre profet wroghte,
Bathe they þat noyes, & þat noyes noghte.
¶ The noyeand, þou made vs for to chasty,
And to clense vs here of owre foly ;   68
And to make vs, to knawe and se,
How febill, & how frele are we ;
The vnnoyeand, to sustayne vs & fede,
& to helpe vs & ese vs in owre nede.   72
Thy creatours are ay whare, in sere stede,
Of whilke, som are qwyke & som are dede ;
For som semes noghte bot als dede thynges,
Als stanes, þat has noghte bot beyngez ;   76
Som, als gryse & treez þat men sese sprynge,
Has beyng & lifynge, bot na felynge.
Som, als bestes þat crepis & rynnys,
& als foghles with fethirs, & fische with fynnes,   80
Hase bathe beyng, lyffyng, & felyng,
Bot na witte ne skyll of demyng.
¶ Som, als men & Angells, has thurghe the
& thurghe þi myghte, beyng & lifyng fre,   84
And feling bath of gude and ill,
And discrecyone of witte and skylle.
Thus has man beyng, als men sese,
With stanes, & lyfe with grysse & treez,   88
And felyng with bestez of sere kynde,
And with Angells skill & mynde.
Thus walde þou, are þou oghte begane,
Þat somwhat of ylke creatoure hade man.   92
Mane, thow made maste dynge creatoure,
& maste semly of schape & of stature,

The four elements,
and all creatures,
for our profit and blessing.

Some things have life, some are without life.

Man, the greatest work

IV. William of Nassington's Poem. God's Mercy.

God made man in His likeness.

Of all oþer creatours mare or lesse,
For þou mad hym aftire thyn owen liknesse   96
And gafe hym lordechipe & powere,
Abowen all oþer vnskillwise creatures sere;
And to rewle hym with witte & skyll,
And for to knawe bathe gud & ill.   100
Whare-fore, gret lufe to man þou kide,
When þou this fore man ordaynede & dide;
It semes þou hade gret lufe tyll man,
Before are þou oghte begane.   104

Nota.

¶ Lorde, I am man for whaym þou dide thus,
And þat man es ilke man & woman of vs;
And als wele all þis þou did for me,
Als for ilk man or woman þat are made thurghe the.

Therefore is he bound to love God.

And for-thy þat I am þat man   109
For whaym þou al thyng begane,
I awe, thurghe ryghte, the to lufe ay,
And to loue the, bathe nyghte & daye,   112
And to wirchipe the with saule & body,
Righte als þou had donne all anely.

[leaf 190.]

Man has a higher blessing than the other creatures, in the Redemption.

Lord God Almyghtty, ȝit thanke I the,
That mekill mare walde doo for me,   116
And all for man-kynd, for thy gudnes,
And thy mercy þat till vs ay redy es,
That fra heuen til erthe down walde com,
To bryng vs here owt of thraledom,   120
And of þe fendis dawngere that we ware In,
Thurghe owre foremaste fadire syn.

Lorde! mekyll þou mekede the for owre sake,
Þat come fra so heghe, owre kynde to take,   124
And vouchede-safe, swa lawe to lighte,
Þat swa heghe a lorde es of grett myghte.
Bot lufe the made, of vs mercy to haue,
Þat fra the was tynt, vs for to saue,   128
Thurghe processe of lyfe þat þou walde lede
In erthe, in oure kynde of manhede.

Firste þou lyghtede in a mayden chayste,   *God born of a Virgin.*
þat conceyuede the of þe Haly Gaste,   132
And of hir body þat was ay wemlesse,
Thow tuke flesche & blude, & oure lyknesse,
And oure kynde here, & of nan oþer,
And be-come mane for vs, and oure brothire;   136
And, for the luffe þou hade till vs,
Walde be borne of hir, & calde Ihesus.
For Ihesus es als mekill for to saye,
Alls hele or helere, þat all hele maye.   140 *Called Jesus Saviour.*
  Thow come to hele vs þat ware lorne,
Bot in na reall place þou was borne,
Nowthire in palays, castell, ne toure,
Ne in non othir stede of honoure,   144
Bot in a lawe hows; and laid þou was   *Born in lowly fashion.*
In a crybe be-fore an Oxe & an asse.
Thow wald nowthir in purpure ne byse
Be lappede, ne in nan oþer clothes of pryce,   148
Bot in vile clowttes, for to couer thi body,
For we sulde take ensample þer-by,
To lufe mekenes & gastely pouerte,
And fra reches & pompes with-draw oure herte.   152
  One þe aughten day of thi byrthe here,   *Circumcised the eighth day.*
That þe firste day es of þe newe ȝere,
Circumsysede in body walde þou be,
Alls þe law was þan in sere contre.   156
In sassyng of þe lawe, and in fullfillyng,
& in Ensampill till vs, & in takenyng,
That als þou was circumsisede in body,
Swa sulde we Circumsise vs here gastely,   160
That es, we sulde schere fra vs away,
All þat til luste & likyng styre vs maye.
  One the twesste day þou was vesete with kynges,
And wirchipede with thre precyous thynges,   164 *Worshipped by kings with three precious gifts.*
That es at say, with golde & Ensence,
And myre, þat þey offerde in þi presence.

Meaning of the gold,
Be þe golde, may vndirstand be
That þou arte kynge of maste pouste; 168
incense,
The Ensence þat þe was offerde nexte,
Be-takyns þat þou art souerayngne priste;
and myrrh.
The myr̄, þat kepis all thynge fra rotyng,
Be-takyns thy dede & þi beryeng. 172

At thirty years old Christ was baptized;
The thritty ȝere of þe Elde of þe,
Of Sayn Iohn wald þou bapteste be,
In þe flom̄ Iourdane specyally,
For to gyfe vs Ensample ther-by, 176
That all sulde be, þat till heuen̄ suld passe,
Baptizede in watyr als þou was;
Bot for na cause of syn̄ in the hyde,
though He never sinned.
Was þou baptizede, þat neuer syn̄ dide; 180
For In the, neuer was funden̄ gyle,
Ne nàthyng þat any saule mypht fyle;
Bot for to lere vs howe we sulde begyn̄
To wesche vs of þe Origenall syn̄, 184
And for to mak vertue in all watirs to be,
For to get vs agayne with grace to be fre.

Tempted in the wilderness.
Sythen̄, when̄ þou had fasted þourghe myghte,
Fourty dayes, & fourty nyghte, 188
Thow sufferd thi selfe, temped to be,
Of þe deuell þat þare-to had leue of the,
To lere vs to wrestyll & stand styfly,
Agayne þe fandyng of þat Enmy. 192
Thow lett the, of Iudas traytour balde,
Betrayed for thirty pieces of silver.
For thritty penys to þe Iewes be saulde;
Thow lette the, alls thefe, be tane bodyly,
Of þe Iewes þat till þe hade Envye, 196
The wilke, till Anna house the ledde,
And than all thi discypills fra þe flede.
Made to suffer indignities.
Till the was don̄ thare at þe begynnyng
Many-fawlde dispyte & hethynge: 200
Firste þey spittede appon̄ þe thare,
And gafe þe many bufettes sare;

And thyne eghne, wit*h* a clathe þey hide,
And smate þe, & askede wha it dide. 204
Sitheñ þey dide þe mare hethyng;   *Sent to Herod and Pilate.*
They lede þe to Herodes hows, þe kyng,
That helde þe a fule, as hym̃ thoghte,
For þou till his speche ansuerde noghte 208
He did clethe þe in whitte garment,
And til Pilate, agayne he þe sente.
Eftirwarde þou was skowreghide sare,   *Scourged.*
In Pilatez hows nakynde bare, 212
That thi hide was all to-reueñ thañ,   [leaf 190 bk.]
And þe blude one ylke a syde dowñ ran*n*e.
The knyghtes, aftire þ*at* skourgegynge,
Abowte þe lappede a mantill in hethynge, 216
That wit*h* þe blude till thi body cleuedè;
Sytheñ drew þey it ofe, & þat þe greuede,
And racede of all þe skyne þat tyde,
For till þat clethynge cleued faste þi hyde. 220
   And wheñ þey had doñ þe þis payne,
They clede þe in þi aweñ clothyng agayne,   *Crowned with thorns.*
And thryste þañ appoñ þi heuede thare,
A Crowne of thornnes þat prykkede þe sare, 224
Of wilke þe prykkes ware swa scharpe þañ,
That þey percede nere thurghe þi her*n*e pan*n*e.
They gafe þe a rede in thi hande,   *With a reed for a sceptre.*
In-stede of a ceptire, the skornande, 228
And knelide be-fore þe in hethynge,
And said till þe 'haile, Iewes kynge!'
Sytheñ was þou demede at þe Iewes voyce,
Thurghe Pilate, to be hynged oñ þe croyce, 232
The wilke þou bare towarde þe stede
Whare þou was ordeynede to be doñ to dede.
Sitheñ was þou straynede oñ þe crosse so faste,   *Mocked and strained on*
Thurghe þe Iewes, þat þi vaynes & synows al to-braste, *the Cross.*
And naylede þ*er*-one, thurghe hand & fute, 237
For hele of my saule, & for my bute.

IV. William of Nassington's Poem. Passion of Jesus.

Crucified.

  And when þey had naylide þe on þe crosse swa,
  They did þe aftire, strange payne & wa,   240
  For they reysede þe crosse with þi body,
  And fychede it in a tre mortasse vyolently,
  In wilke, þe crosse swilke a Iage tuke,
  Þat þi body, thurghe weghte al to-schoke.   244
  Than raue thy wondes thurghe fute & hande,
  And ware sene full wyde gapaunde,
  And þe Ioynetes of ilk lym & bane,
  And þe vaynes ware strydand ilkane.   248

Cries 'I thirst.'

  Sithen þou said, hyngande on þe rude tree,
  The thristede, and þan þe Iewes bed the

Given gall and vinegar.

  A full bittire drynke, þat was wroghte
  Of ayscll & gall, þat þe lykede noghte;   252
  Neuer-þe-lattere, to taste it þou was bown,
  Bot þou walde noghte swelowe it down,
  For þat thriste was noghte ells þan,
  Bot a ȝernynge aftyre þe sawle of man.   256

Reproved by a thief and by Jews.

  Thow suffirde many repreues þat tyde,
  Bathe on þe thefe þat hange on þi lefte syde,
  And of othire maysters of þe Iewry,
  That mekill schame þe dide, & velany.   260

Cries 'Eli, Eli.'

  At nonne of the daye þou cryed 'Hely,'
  & ȝeldide þi gaste to þi fadir Almyghty.

Dies;

  Thus þou diede, to make vs free
  Fra þe grett thraldome in whilke ware we.   264
  Bot mekill payne & mekill reprefe,
  Þou tholed before þi dede, fore oure lufe;

for our deliverance and example.

  And noghte for to bye vs agayne anely,—
  For why þi dede moghte suffyce vs all to bye,— 268
  Bot for we sulde þare-by Ensampill take,
  To be pacyente in angers for þi sake,
  And for the to thole all þat harde es,
  Alls þou tholede for vs, thurghe þi gudnes.   272
  Ells thurte þe hafe tholede nan oþer payne
  Bot þe dede anely, for to bye vs agayne.

Sythen was þou smetyn in þi reghte syde — Christ's side pierced.
With a spere, þat till þi herte gun glide,   276
Fra whilke owte rane, to oure saluacyone,
The precyous blode of owre raunsonne,
With þe water of baptym, clere & thyn,
For to wesche vs here of þe Oregynall syn.   280
¶ Lorde, for þire bitter paynes & fell,
With othire ma þat I kane tell,
That þou swa mekill suffire walde — Praise to the Saviour for his mercy.
For me synfull, þi traytoure baulde,   284
I thanke þe here Inwardly,
With all my herte and my body.
¶ A, Ihesu Crist! Lorde, full of myghte, ¶ Nota. — The unworthiness and sinfulness of man.
When I thynke, outhire day or nyghte,   288
Of swa mekill kyndnes of þe,
And of þe paynes þat þou tholide for me,
And of myn vnkyndnesse many-fawlde,
& how I to wrethe the ay hafe bene bawlde,   292
Of myn hard herte þan es grete wondire,
Þat it for sorowe bristez noghte In sundyre.
Bot flescly herte in me semes nan,
For my herte es hard als it ware stane.   296 — My heart is as hard as stone.
¶ A, Jhesu! I grante to þe my trespas,
And knawes þat I am wers þan Iudas was,
That the bytrayede als traytoure balde,
& til þe Iewes, for thritty penys sawlde.   300
For I, synfull wreche, has ofte sawlde the
For a littill worldly vanyte,
And for a littill fleschely delyte,
Whare-fore I am mare þan Iudas to wyte.   304
I halde me ȝitt werse, & mare wode
Þan þe Iewes ware þat did þe one þe rude; — Christ crucified again by sin.
For why þay dide þe bot anes þat dede,
& þey knewe þe noghte Gode in manhede;   308
And I, þat wate & knawes righte
Þat þou arte Gode ay full of myghte,

Thurghe mynͩ awenͩ malece, as I ware wode,
Fuȴȴ ofte sythes hafe I donͩ þe one þe rude. 312
[leaf 191.]
For, als ofte als I hafe done dedly synͩ,
And thurghe malece wetandly fallynͩ there-Inͩ,
Alls ofte hafe I done þe one þe rude,
In þat þat in me was, and schede þi blude. 316
Lorde! aȴȴ if I hafe done swilke foly,

Prayer for mercy.
Putt me noghte away fra þi mercy,
Bot graunte me grace þat may me wysse
To amende me of þat, I hafe donne mysse; 320
Sen þat þou saide þi selfe, þou wiȴȴ noghte
The dede of synfuȴȴ þat þou has boghte,
Bot þat he turne hymͩ to doo þi wiȴȴ,
And lyfe, for þou wiȴȴ na man spyȴȴ, 324
Lorde! swylke grace þou me gyffe,
Þat I may turne me to þe, and lyffe!

A, Lord Ihesu Criste, ȝit thanke I the,
Þat aȴȴ þis, & mare, has done for me, 328
And for saluacyone of mankynde,
For whaymͩ þou was swa bitterly pynede,
And sufferde dede, als I be-for saide,

Christ descended into hell.
And lett þi body be in sepulcre layde. 332
Thow ȝernede sa mekiȴȴ agayne to wyne
Aȴȴ þas þat þou hade loste for synͩ,
That whenͩ þow was dede, & ȝeldede þe gaste,
Als tyte tiȴȴ heȴȴ þou gun þe haste, 336
In saule & godhede, als was þi wiȴȴ,
Thy body whils in þe sepulcre lay styȴȴ;
Till þou at heȴȴ come, þou walde noghte stynte,
& ware sesede of þas þat þou hade tynte. 340

And spoiled it of his.
Thow spoylede heȴȴ whenͩ þou come þare,
And tuke owt with the, aȴȴ þat thyne ware.
Bot þou lefte þas pare þat walde noghte trowe
In þi lawe, ne in þi biddynge bowe. 344

Rose again the third day.
Sythenͩ, when þou come fra þat stede,
At þe thred day aftyre þi dede,

To vpe-ryse fra dede þou vouchede-safe,
To eke þe trowhe þat we here hafe, 348
And schewede the bodily in thi manhede,
To conferme þe trowthe for oure mede.
Whare-fore þi bodily vp-ryssynge,   *All men shall rise in their*
Till vs Ensample es, and takynnynge, 352 *bodies,*
That we sall ryse all generally
At þe day of dome, in saule & bodye.
Thane sall all þat are fundyn reghtewisse,
Thurghe thyn vprysynge, to blysse ryse; 356
Bot þay þat lyffes ill vn-to þeire Endynge,
Gettes na parte of thyn vpe-rysynge;
Bot þay sall ryse with dule þat day,
Till þe fire of hell, þat lastes aye. 360 *and go either to Hell or Bliss.*
ȝitt thi rysyng, forbysen till vs es,
For all þat rase fra dede til blyse Endlesse,
Swa sulde we þat til blysse will wyn,
Gastely ryse fra dedely syn. 364

    Eftire þi rysesynge, als þe buke sais,   *Christ, risen, remained on*
Þou duellede in erthe ȝitt fourtty dayes, *earth forty days.*
And at þe fourtty day þou stey vp-righte
Til þi fader, in-till heuen bryghte,— 368 *Ascended into heaven.*
To teche vs þe way þat we sall wende,
Til þe gret blysse þat has nan Ende,—
And sittis þare, one þi Fadire reghte hande,
Als God & Lorde alweldande, 372
That es to saye, in Godhede euen
With thi Fadir & owrs in heuen.

    The tendaye aftire þat þou vp wente,   *On the tenth day after, the*
At vndrone þe Haly Gaste down þou sente 376 *Holy Ghost came down,*
Till thyn Appostills, als þou þem hyghte,
Þat þeire hertes comforthede, & made þem lyghte,
Thurghe whame lyghtenede & leride ware we:
Off all þis, Lorde, I thanke þe. 380

    A, Lorde Ihesu! at þe dredfull daye of domme, *Christ shall come again to*
When þou sall fra heuen come *judgment,*

With thyne angells bryghte & clere,
And Apostells & oþer halowes sere, 384
In þe same fourme of man, and lyknesse,
In wilke þou was demyde here giltlesse,—

to judge the good and bad.

To deme gud & ill of ilke lande,
Schewande þi wondes al bledande, 388
That þou walde thole for synfull mane—

The strict account that must be given then.

What sall I say, or what sall I do þan?
When all oure werkes þat euer we dyde,
Sall þan be schewede, & nathyng hide, 392
Of whilke we sall ȝelde a-cownte straitly,
And be demyde aftire we are worthi.
And I, than with me na gud sall brynge
Be-fore sa heghe domesman & kynge, 396
Bot synnez þat are swa manyfaulde,
That þey may noghte by tonge be tawlde;
Certes I am þare-fore full dredand;
My herte, for dred aghte to be full tremblande, 400
When discussione sall be of all dedis,
And þi wrethe sall be maste þat all men dredis.

Then can we only utter the prayer of David.

Certes I ne wate whate I may say þan,
Bot alls Dauid did, þe haly man: 404
'Do þou, Lorde, with þi seruande,
Eftyre þi mercy, þat es ay sauande;
And in-till dome come þou noghte
With þi seruande þat þou has boghte.' 408
For I hafe hade grete drede in thoghte
Of þi domes, and þat drede leffe I noghte;

leaf 191 bk.]

For þou, Lorde, arte reghtewysse domes-mane,
That all thyng reghtewissly dem kane. 412
And thi reghtwysse dome & reghtwyssnes
Domes synfull men to payne Endlesse,
That of þeyre wikkidnesse will noghte blyn,
And þi mercy here may nott wyn. 416

None can be saved who has not obtained Christ's mercy here,

For sekere, of mercy nane getes he,
In þis life bot he turne hym till þe;

And nane may þat daye be saffe,
Bot he þi mercy in þis lyfe hafe,   420
Of whilke þou erte large & leberall,   *which He will grant to all who ask it.*
To grante it bathe grete & smalle,
That mercy askes, & folowes þare-to,
And dos þare-fore þat þem falles to doo.   424

Whare-fore, Lorde, sen þou arte ay redy   *Lord, grant me Thy mercy now!*
To graunte till ilke a man þi mercy,
That sekes þar-to whils þay here lyffe,
Swilke grace in þis lyfe þou me gyffe,   428
To turne me, and to fle syn;
Þat I may here þi mercy wyn, Amen,
Thurghe whilke I may, at þe dredfull day,
Be led to þe blyse þat sall last ay. Amen!   432

V.
THANKS TO CHRIST FOR HIS MERCIES.

[Robert Thornton's MS., Linc. Cath., on leaf 191 bk.]

Lorde Gode Ihesu cryste, Godd Almyghty,   *Christ, I thank Thee for creating me,*
   I thanke þe with all my herte hally
     That me, man, schope and mad of noghte,
     And of vile matere me furthe broghte;   4
And my body, swa made of vile matere,
Thow knyttide to-gedire in Ioyntes sere,
And my sawle made, thurghe thyn Inspayre,   *my soul,*
& gaffe me lymmes semly & faire.   8
Fra a myrke downgeon þou broghte me righte,
Þat es, my modirs wambe, to þis lighte,
And Efte gate me, as þi barne newe borne thurghe baptym,
Þat was þe fendes childe lorne;   12
And fyve wittes of body þou has gyffen me,   *and my five wits.*
And skyll, ware-with þey sulde rewlyde bee;
And all, if I hafe done agayns þi lawe,
Thi gudes þou will noghte fra me drawe,   16

V. Thanks to Christ for His Mercies.

<small>And though I sin against Thee daily, Thou sendest me my food and clothes,</small>

That a false traytoure aganes þe es ay,
And trespes agayne the here ilke daye.
Thow sendes me here, thurghe þi purueance,
Ilke daye my nedefull sustenance, 20
That es to saye, met & clathe fre,
And all þat nedfull es to me.
Thow has tholede me, & venged þe noghte
of my syn þat I hafe agayne þe wroghte, 24
And ȝitt suffers & gyffes me space
to turne me to þe, & take þi grace;

<small>and when I have fallen in the devil's power, Thou sparest me, and hast</small>

And ay when I hafe fallyn in the fendis bawndon,
Þou has sauede me fra fynall dampnacyon, 28
That I ware for my wikkidnes worthy;
bot þou has couerde me with þi mercy,
And ay has sparede me, & ȝitt spares,
And kepes me fra þe deuyllis snares, 32
And agayne his darttes has bene my schelde,

<small>saved me from many dangers.</small>

And has sauede me, bathe in ȝouthe & elde,
Fra many perells in many sere stedis,
And fra myschance & sudayne dedes. 36

<small>For these and all other benefits, I thank Thee, and pray Thee for Thy grace to mend my life, and live in bliss with Thee.</small>

For all thes þat I hafe rehersede here,
And for all oþer gudes & benfettes sere
That thow till me, synfull caytife,
hase gracyousely done in þis lyfe, 40
I thanke þe, Lorde, with all louyng,
And prayes þe þou take me in thi kepyng,
And saue me forthewarde as þou has done,
And graunte me þi grace, whills I here wonne, 44
To mende my lyfe, & lyfe in clennes,
Þat I may wonne with þe in blisse Endlesse. Amen! 46

VI. A PRAYER TO CHRIST. [on leaf 191 bk.]

(1)

Almighty God in trinite,
   Inwardly I thanke þe
   For thy gud ded þat þou me wroghte,
And with þi precyous blude me boghte,   4
And of all gud þat þou lennes me.
Lorde, blyssede mott þou be!
Honour, Ioye & louyng
Be til þi name with-owttyn endyng! Amen!   8

God, I thank Thee for the good Thou givest me.

(2)

Lorde God alweldande,
I beteche to-daye into þi hande,
my sawle & my body,
And all my Frendes specyally,   12
Bathe þe quik and þe dede:
graunt them parte of my bede!
Kepe vs all in erthe here,—
Fore þe prayere of thi modyr dere,   16
And all thy haloghes þat are in heuen,—
Fra þe dedly synnes seuen,
And fra fandyng of þe euyll wyghte,
And Fra sodayne dede, bathe daye & nyghte!   20

I commit to Thy hands myself and my friends.

Keep us from sin,

(3)

Schelde us fra þe paynes of hell,
þat bitter are to thole, & ffell,
And with thi grace fulfill vs all,
Þat redy we may be to þi call;   24
And late vs neuer parte fra þe,
Alls thow for vs died one a tree!
Graunte vs, Lorde, þat [it] swa bee!
Amen! Amen, pur charite!   28

and the pains of Hell,

and let us never part from Thee!

VII. A PRAYER FOR MERCY.

(1)

<small>Jesu, have mercy on me!</small>

Ihesu, that diede one the rude for þe lufe of me,
 And boghte me with thi precious blode, Thow hafe mercy of me!

<small>[leaf 192.]</small>

Whatt me lettes of any thyng for to luffe the,
Be it me lefe, be it me lathe, do it awaye fra me!   4

(2)

Ihesu, of whayme all trewe luffe sprynges,
 That for my lufe tholede payne,
Till lusty lufe of erthely thynges

<small>Let me not turn again to love of earth, but make me joy in Thy love.</small>

 Thow thole me neuer turne agayne!   8
In thi luffe be my likynge,
 And there-to make me glade & fayne,
And for thy lufe to make mournynge,
 That for my lufe walde be slayne.   12
   Amen! Amen! Amen! Amen, pur **charite!**

[Then comes the prose treatise, 'Of the vertuȝ of the haly name of Ihesu,' printed in Hampole's Prose Treatises, E. E. T. Soc., p. 1, &c.]

VIII. FIRST HYMN TO JESUS CHRIST.

[21 alternates of 4 : *ab ab*.]

(1)   [on leaf 211.]

Ihesu Criste, Saynte Marye sonne,   Jesus!
    Thurgh whaym þis werlde was worthily wroghte,
I pray þe come, and in me wonne,   Dwell in me,
    And of all filthes clense my thoghte.   4

(2)

Ihesu Criste, my Godde verray,
    Þat of oure dere Lady was borne,
Þou helpe now, and euer and aye,   help me,
    And lat me neuer for syn be lorne!   8

(3)

Ihesu Criste, Goddes sone of heuene,
    Þat for me dyede one þe rude,
I pray þe here my symple steuene,
    Thurghe þe vertue of thi haly blude.   12

(4)

Ihesu Criste, þat one þe thirde daye,
    Fra dede to lyffe rase thurgh thi myghte,
Þou gyffe me grace the serue to paye,   give me grace,
    And þe to wirchipe, day and nyghte.   16

(5)

Ihesu, of whaym all gudnes sprynges,
    Whaym all men awe to lufe by righte,   [leaf 211, col. 2.]
Thou make me to ȝeme thi biddynges,   to fulfil thy biddings!
    And thaym fullfill with all my myghte!   20

VIII. *First Hymn to Christ.*

(6)
Ihesu Crist, þat tholede for me
    Paynes & angers, bitter & felle,
Late me neuer be partede fra þe,
    Ne thole þe bitter paynes of helle!   24

Let me not suffer in Hell!

(7)
Ihesu Criste, welle of mercy,
    Of pete and of all gudnes,
Of all þe synnes þat euer did I,
    I pray þe gyffe me forgyffnes!   28

Jesus! forgive my sins,

(8)
Ihesu, to þe I make my mane;
    Ihesu, to þe I calle and crye,
Late neuer my saule with syn be slane,
    For þe mekillnes of þi mercy!   32

(9)
Ihesu, þat es my saueoure,
    Þou be my Ioy and my solace,
My helpe, my hele, my comfortoure,
    And my socoure in ilke a place!   36

be my joy,

[leaf 211 bk.]

(10)
Ihesu, þat with thi blude me boghte,
    Ihesu, þou make me clene of syn,
And with þi lufe þou wounde my thoghte,
    And late me neuer-mare fra þe twynne!   40

cleanse me,

(11)
Ihesu, I couayte to lufe the,
    And þat es hally my ȝernynge,
Þare-fore, to lufe þe, þou lere me,
    And I thi lufe sall [euer] synge.   44

(12)
Ihesu, thi lufe in-to me sende,
    And with þi lufe þou me Fede!
Ihesu, þi lufe ay in me lende!
    Thi lufe euer be my saule mede   48

feed me with Thy love!

VIII. *The Soul Seeking Jesus.*   81

(13)
Ihesu, my herte with lufe þou lyghte!   Light my
    Thi lufe, me make euer to forsake   heart with
All werldly Ioy, bathe day & nyghte,   love of Thee;
    And Ioy in þe anely to make!   52

(14)
Ihesu, þi lufe me chaufe with-in,
    So þat na thynge bot the I seke!
In thi lufe make my saule to brynne;
    Thi lufe me make bathe milde and meke!   56   and make me meek and mild!

(15)
Ihesu, my Ioy and my louynge,   Jesus! join
    Ihesu, my comforthe clere,
Ihesu my Godde, Ihesu my kynge,
    Ihesu withowtten pere,   60

(16)
Ihesu, þat all hase made of noghte,
    Ihesu, þat boghte me dere,
Ihesu, Ioyne þi lufe in my thoghte.   the love of Thee with my
    Swa þat þay neuer be sere!   64   mind!

(17)
Ihesu, my dere, & my drewrye,
    Delyte þou arte to synge;
Ihesu, my myrthe, and my melodye,
    In-to thi lufe me brynge!   68

(18)
Ihesu, Ihesu, my hony swete,
    My herte, my comforthynge,
Ihesu, all my bales þou bete,
    And to þi blysse me brynge!   72   Bring me to Thy bliss!

(19)
Ihesu, in thi lufe wounde my thoghte,
    And lyfte my herte to the!
Ihesu, my saule þat þou dere boghte,
    Thi lufere, mak it to bee!   76

VIII. *First Hymn to Christ.*

(20)

<small>Give me Grace,</small>

Now, Ihesu Lorde, þou gyffe me grace,
   If it be thi wilt,
That I may come vn-to þi place,

<small>to dwell ever with Thee!</small>

   And wonn ay with the stylle. Amen! 80

Explicit **T**ractatus. **Explicit. Ameñ. Thornton. Ameñ.**

IX HYMN TO JESUS CHRIST AND THE VIRGIN

[13 Stanzas, 2 of 6 lines, 11 of 8 : *ab ab ab ab.*]   [leaf 211 bk., col. 2.]

(1)

Fadir, and Son, and Haly Gaste,
    Lorde, to þe I make my mone,
Stedfaste kyng of myghtës maste,
    Alle-weldand Gode sittand in trone.   4
I praye þe, Lorde, þat þou þe haste
    To for-gyffe þat I hafe mysdone.   6

God, Three in One,

(2)

Lorde, hafe mercy of my syn,
    And brynge me owte of all my care!   8
Euylle to doo, I couthe neuer blyn,
    I hafe ay wroghte agaynes þi lare.
Þou rewe one me bathe owte and In,
    And hele me of my woundës sare!   12

have mercy on me!

(3)

Fadir of Heuen, þat all may,   13
    I pray þe, Lorde, þat þou me lede,
In stabyll trouthe þe ryghtë way,
    At myn Endynge, when I sall drede.   16
Thi grace I aske, bathe nyghte & day,
    Hafe mercy now of my mysdedez!
Of myn askynge, say me noghte nay,
    Bot helpe me, Lorde, att all my nede   20

Lead me in the right way!

IX. Hymn to Christ and the Virgin. Her Intercession.

(4)

Jesus! let me

Swete Ihesu þat for me was borne,
 Þou here my prayere loude and stille,
For paynes þat me ere laide beforne,
 Full ofte I syghe, and wepis my fylle, 24
Full ofte haf I bene forswourne,
 When I hafe wroghte agaynes þi will;

not be lost for my ill deeds!

Thou late me neuer be forlorne,
 Lorde, for my dedis ille! 28

(5)

Holy Ghost!

Haly Gaste, I pray to the,
 Nyghte and day with gud entente,

comfort me!

In all my sorowe þou comforthe me,
 Thi haly grace be to me sente; 32
And late me neuer bownden bee
 In dedly syn, þat I be schente,
For Marie lufe, þat mayden free,
 In whaym þou lyghtë verraymente. 36

(6)

Mary, lady!

I pray the, Lady, meke and mylde,
 Þat þou pray for my misdede,
For þe luffe of þat ilke childe,
 Þat þou saghe one þe rudë blede. 40
Ewire & ay haf I bene wylde,

[leaf 212.]

 My synfull saule es euer in drede;
Mercy, Lady, meke and mylde!

help me in my need!

 Þou helpe me euer, at all my nede! 44

(7)

Mercy, Mary, mayden clene!
 Þou late me neuer in syn duelle,
Pray for me, þat it be sene,

Shield me from the fire of Hell!

 And schelde me fra þe fyre of helle! 48
Certis, Lady, wele I wene
 Þat all my faamen may þou felle;

IX. Man's Need of Help.

For-þi, my sorowe to þe I mene;
  With drery mode my tale I telle.   52

(8)

Bethynke þe, Lady, euer and ay,   Mary! counsel
  Þat of women þou beris þe flour,
For synfull men, als I þe say,
  Oure Lorde hase done þe gret honour.   56
Helpe me, Lady, so wele þou may!
  Þe behouse be my consailloure;
Of consaile, Lady, I þe praye,
  And also of helpe & of socoure.   60   and help me!

(9)

Nyghte and day, in wele & wa,
  In all my sorowe, þou comforthe me,   Comfort me
And be my schelde agayne my faa;
  And kepe me, gyffe þi willes bee,   64   and keep me from sin!
Fra dedly syn þat will me slaa!
  Mercy, Lady, faire and Free,
Þou take þat þe es fallen fraa,
  For thi mercy and þi pete!   68

(10)

At myn Endynge þou stand by me,   Stand by me when I die!
  Heyn when I sall founde and Fare,
When I sall qwake, and dredfull be,
  And all my synnës sowe full sare.   72
Als ay my hope hase bene in the,
  I pray þe, Lady, helpe me þare,
For þe luffe of þe swette tre,
  Þat Ihesu sprede one, his body bare.   76

(11)

Ihesu, for þat ilke hardë stounde,   Jesus! have
  Þat þou walde one þe rude tre blede,
At myne Endynge, when I sall founde,
  Hafe mercy, Lorde, of my mysdede!   80   mercy on me!

And helpe me þare of þe dedes wounde,
 And kepe me þare at all my nede!
When dede me takes, & brynges to grounde,
 Lorde, þare I sall thi domës drede.   84

(12)

[leaf 212, col. 2.]
Grant me time for repentance!

For my synnes to do penance
 Be-fore my dede, Lorde, graunt þou me,
And space of verray répentance
 Inwardly I beseke the.   88
In thi mercy es my fyaunce,
 Of my foly þou hafe peté,
And of me take þou na vengeance,
 Lorde, for þi debonerte!   92

(13)

Lorde, als þou erte full of myghte,
 Whase lufe es swetteste for to taste,
My lyfe amende, My dedis þou ryghte,
 For Marie lufe, þe mayden chaste!   96

Bring me to the sight of Thee, God, Three in One!

And brynge me to þat ilkë syghte,
 One þe to see, þare Ioy es maste,
One þe to see þat Ioyfull syghte,
 Fadir, and Sonn, and þe Haly Gaste. Amen!   100

Explicit[1] &c.

[1] With a flourish like 'ff'.

X. A PRAYER TO CHRIST.

[On lf. 212, col. 2.]

Ihesu Criste, Goddes sun of heuen, kyng of kynges, and lorde of lordes, mi lorde, and my Godd! For þe mekenes of þi clene incarnacione, and thurghe þe meryte of þi harde passione, Safe vs fra dampnacione, Socoure vs in temptacione, and gyffe vs thi benysone, and of all oure wykkidnes playne perdone and full remyssione, thurgh verray contrission, nakede confessione, and worthi satisfaccione! Graunte vs alswa, Lorde Godd, in heuen ay-lastande mansione and euer to se þe cherefull visione of thi faire face, for þe lufe þat þou schewede to mankynde! Amen! *Save us from damnation, forgive our sins, and let us see thy face!*

Explicit.

[Follows, 'A [Latin] Meditacione of þe Fyve woundes of oure Lorde Ihesu Criste, *with* a prayere in þe same.' *Adoro te, piissime Ihesu, qui redemisti me* . . .

Then, on lf. 212 bk. col. 2, 'A [Latin] Medytacion of the Crosse of Criste, *with* a prayere'—*O crux frutex* . . .].

XI. MORAL POEM: WITH I. AND E.

[Eight Stanzas of 12 lines each : *ab ab* (or *cb*) *ab ab fh gh.*]

(1)

[leaf 213.]
When Adam dug, and Eve span, where was man's pride?

When Adam dalfe, and Euë spane,
    Go spire, if þou may spede,
Whare was þaɴ þe pride of maɴ,
    Þat nowe merres his mede?   4
Of erthe and lame, as was Adam,
    Nakede to noye and nede,
We er, als he, maked to be,
    Whills we þis lyfe sall lede.   8
With I and E, borne er we,
    As Salamoɴ vs highte,
To trauell here whills we er fere,
    As fewle vn-to þe flyghte.   12

(2)

We were destined to trouble, to weal or woe.

In werlde we ware casteɴ for care,
    To we ware worthi to wende
To wele or wa, ane of þase twa,
    To welde *with*-owtteɴ ende.   16
For-thi, whills þou may helpe þe nowe,

Reform now !
    Amend þe, & hafe mynde[1],
When þou sall ga, he bese thi Faa,
    Þat here was are thi Frende.   20

[1] The ryme needs 'mende.'

With E and I, I rede forthi,
  Vmthynke þe ay of thre,
What we er, and whate we warre,
  And whate þat we sall be.   24   Think of what we are, were, and shall be.

        (3)
Ware þou als wysse, praysede in pryce,   If you were as wise as Solomon,
  Als was Salomon,
Wele fairere fude of bane & blude,
  Þat was Absolon,   28
Strenghely and strange, to wreke thi wrang as strong as Sampson,
  As euer was Sampson,
Þou ne myghte, a day, na mare þan þay,
  Þe dede with-stand allone.   32   you couldn't resist Death.
With I and E, þe dede to þe,
  Sall com als I þe ken,
Bot þou ne wate in whatekyn state
  Ne how, ne whare, ne whenne.   36

        (4)
When bemes sall blawe, rewly one rawe,
  To rekkenynge buse vs ryse,   We must rise for Judgment,
When he sall comme vn-to þat domme
  Ihesu to sitt Iustyse.   40
Þat are was leue, þane mon be greue,
  When all gastis sall ryse,
I say þat pan, to synfull man,
  Sary bese þat assise.   44
With I and E, he sall noghte flee,
  If all he his giltes fele,   and cannot hide.
He ne may hym hide, bot þare habyde,
  Ne fra þat dome appelle.   48

        (5)
Of all thyne aughte, þat þe was raughte,
  Sall þou noghte hafe, I hete,
Bot seuen fote, þare-in to rote,   7 foot to rot in, is all we shall have.
  And a wyndynge schete.   52

For-þi þou gyffe, whils þou may lyfe,
  Or all gase þat þou may gete,
Thi gaste fra Godd, þi gudes o lodde,
  Thi flesche foldes vndir fete. 56
With I and E, full sekire þou be,
  þat thynne executurs.
Of þe ne will rekke, bot skikk ande skekke
  Full baldely in thi boures. 60

(6)

To dome we drawe, þe sothe to schawe,
  In lyfe þat vs was lente.
No latyn ne lawe, may helpe an hawe,
  Bot rathely vs repente. 64
The croice, þe crownne, þe spere bese bowne,
  þat Ihesu ruggede & rente;
þe nayles ruyde sall þe eonclude
  With thyne awen argument. 68
With E, and O, take kepe þare-to,
  As Criste hym-selfe vs kende;
We comme and goo, to wele or wo,
  That dredfull dome sall ende. 72

(7)

Of will and witt þat vesettis it
  In worde, and þat we wroghte,
Rekken we mon, and ȝelde reson
  Full rathely of our thoghte. 76
Sall no fallace cufere our case,
  Ne consaile gette we noghte;
No gyfte ne grace, noþer þare gase,
  Bot brwke as we hafe broghte. 80
With E and I, I rede for-thi,
  Be warre nowe with thi werkes,
For terymes of ȝere, hase þou nane here,
  Thi medes sall be thi merkes. 84

(8)

What so it be, þat we here see,
   Þe fairehede of thi face, *No beauty 'll avail us,*
Thi ble so bryghte, thi mayne, thi myghte,
   Þi mouthe þat myrthis mase. 88
All mon als was, to powdir passe, *All goes in the grave.*
   To graue when þat þou gase,
A grysely geste, þan bese þou preste,
   In armës for to brace. 92
With I and E, for leue þou me,
   Bese nane, as I þe hete,
Of all þi kyth dare slepe þe with, *In the grave no kinsman*
   A nyghte vndir þi schete. 96 *'ll dare sleep with you.*

Sit nomen Domini benedictum, ex hoc nunc, et usque in seculum! Amen!

XII. A PRAYER TO JESUS.

Ihesu Criste, have mercy one me, [on leaf 213 bk.]
Als þou erte kynge of mageste, *Jesus,*
And forgiffe me my synnes all, *forgive my sins, and*
Þat I hafe donne, bathe grete and small,
And brynge me, if it be thi will, *bring me to heaven.*
Till heuen to wonn ay with þe styll! Amen!

[Follows, 'A sermon þat Dan Iohn Gaytrye made,' printed above, pp. 1–15, to the end of leaf 218 of the MS.]

XIII. A SECOND HYMN TO JESUS CHRIST.

[Thirteen Stanzas of 8 lines: *ab* (or *cb*) *ab ab ab*; and one, St. (7), of 9 lines: *ab aab ab ab*.]

(1)

[leaf 219.]
If we knew Jesus' sweetness, earthly love would be bitter.

IHesu, thi swetnes, wha moghte it se
    And þare-of hafe a clere knaweynge,
Aƚƚ erthely lufe sulde bitter bee,
    Bot thyne allane, with-owtteñ lesynge.   4
I pray þe, Lorde, þat lare lere mee,
    Aftir þi lufe to hafe langynge,
And sadly sett my herte one þe,
    In þi lufe to hafe lykynge.   8

(2)

So lykand lufe, in erthe nane es,
    In saule, wha-sa couthe hertly se,
To lufe hym wele, ware mekill blysse,

He is King of Love.

    For, 'kyng of lufe,' callede es he.   12
With trewe lufe, I walde, I-wysse,
    So harde to hym, bowndeñ be,
Þat my herte ware hally hys,
    And oþer lufe lykede noghte me.   16

(3)

If I, for kyndnes, suld luf my kyñ,
    Ay me thynke þus in my thoghte,
By kyndly skyƚƚ I sulde be-gyñ
    At hym, þat me, guñ make of noghte.   20

He has set his likeness in my soul.

Hys semblant he sette my saule with-in,
    And this werlde, for me he wroghte,

XIII. *Second Hymn to Jesus Christ.*

As fadir of fude, my lufe to wyne,
    For herytage in heuen̄, he me boghte.   24

(4)

As modir, of hym̄ I may make mynde,   *He cared for me before I was born, He is my Mother,*
    Þat, are my byrthe, to me tuke hede,
And seyn̄ with baptym̄ weschede þat strynde,
    With synn̄ was fylede with Adames dede.   28
With nobill mete he nureschede my kynde,
    For with his flesche he walde me fede;
A better fude may na man̄ fynde,
    For, to lastande lyfe it will vs lede.   32

(5)

My broþer and syster he es by skyll,   *my Brother and Sister.*
    For he saide, & lerede þat lare,
Þat wha-sa dide his fadyr will,
    Systers and breþer till hym þay ware.   36
My kynde also he tuke þare till;
    Full trewly I tryste þare-fore,
Þat he will neuer lat me spyll,
    Bot with his mercy sane my sore.   40   *He will save me.*

(6)

Eftyr his lufe me bude lange,
    For he has myn̄, full dere boghte,[1]   *[leaf 219, col. 2.]*
When I was went fra hym with wrange,
    Fra heuen̄ to erthë, he me soghte.   44   *He sought me from Heaven, and suffered for me.*
My wrechede kynde, for me he fange,
    And all his noblay sette at noghte;
Pouerte he suffirde, & penance strange,
    To blysse agayne are he me broghte.   48

(7)

When̄ I was thralle, to make me fre,
    Mi lufe fra heuen̄ till erthe hym ledde,

---

[1] This line was first written thus:—
    'For he has boghte myn full dere.'

XIII. Second Hymn to Jesus Christ.

My lufe allanë, hafe walde he,
    And þat my saule sulde sauede bee. 52
Þare-fore he laide his lyfe in wedde;
He fought my foe for me.   With my faa, he faughte for mee;
Woundide he was, & bitterly bledde:
    His precyous blude, full of plentee, 56
Full petevofely for me was schede. 57

(8)

He bled for me. ¶ His sydes full bla and bludy ware, 58
    That sumtym̄ ware full brighte of blee,
His herte was perchede with a spere,
    His bludy woundes was reuthe to see. 61
My raunson̄ I-wys he payede þare,
He gave His life for my sin,   And gaffe his lyffe for gylte of me,
His dulefull dede burde do me dere,
    And perche myn̄ herte for pure petee. 65

(9)

¶ For pete myn̄ herte burde breke in two,
    To his kyndenes, if I tuke hede;
Encheson̄ I was, of all his wo;
    He sufferde full harde for my mysdede. 69
to win me eternal Life, To lastand lyfe, for I sulde goo,
    The dede he tholede in his manhede,
When his will was to lyfe also,
    He rasse agayne thurghe his Godhede. 73

(10)

¶ Till heuen̄ he wente with mekill blysse
    When̄ he hade venqwyste his bataile;
His banere full brade displayede es,
    When so my faa will me assaile. 77
Wele aghte myn̄ herte þan to be his,
    For he es þat frende þat neuer will faile,
and he wants nothing but my love. And, na thynge he will I-wys,
    Bot trewe lufe for his trauaile. 81

XIII. *Second Hymn to Jesus Christ.*

(11)

¶ Thus walde my spousë for me fyghte,   [leaf 219 bk.]
   And woundide for me, he was full sare,
For my lufe his dede was dyghte:
   What kyndnes myghte he do me mare?   85
To ȝelde hym his' lufe, hafe I na myghte,
   Bot lufe hym lelly, I sulde þare-fore,   *And I ought to love Him loyally.*
And wyrke his will with werkës ryghte,
   That he me leryde with lufely lore.   89

(12)

¶ His lufly lare with werkes fulfill,
   Wele aghte me, wreche, if I ware kynde,   *I ought to do His will,*
Nyghte and daye to wirke his will,
   And euer-mare hafe hym in mynde.   93
Bot gastely Enemyse greues me ill,
   And my frele fleschë makes me blynde,   *but my flesh is frail.*
Thare-fore his mercy, I take me till,
   For bettire bute, I kane nane fynde.   97

(13)

¶ Bettire bute es nane to me,
   Bot till his mercy trewely me take,   *I trust His mercy,*
That with his budë made me fre,
   And me, a wreche, his sun walde make.   101
I praye þat Lorde, for his pete,   *pray for His pity.*
   For my synn, noghte me for-sake,
Bot gyffe me grace, syn for to flee,
   And in his lufe lat me neuer slake.   105

(14)

A, Ihesu! for þe swetnes þat in the es,   *Ah, Jesu! When I die,*
   Hafe mynde of me when I sall wende!
With stedfaste trouthe my wittës wysse,
   And defende me, fra þe fende!   109   *defend,*

XIII. *Second Hymn to Jesus Christ.*

<small>forgive me!</small>   For þi mercy, forgyffe me my mysse,
              That wikkede werkes, my saule ne schende,
<small>bring me to Thy bliss.</small> Bot brynge me, Lorde, vnto þi blysse,
              With þe to wonn with-owtten ende. Amen! 113
              Explicit.

[Follows, the prose treatise on 'The Anehede of Godd with Manns Saule,' printed in Hampole's Prose Treatises, E. E. T. Soc. 1866, pp. 14–19. Then the poem 'Þi Ioy be, ilke a dele, to serue thi Godd to paye,' printed below, p. 107.]

XIV.

[*Thornton MS.*, lf. 231.]

¶ Of Sayne Iohn þe Euaungelist.

(Nineteen Stanzas of 14 lines each : *ab ab ab ab, ccd, ccd.*)

(1)

OF all mankynde þat he made, þat maste es of myghte,   Of all men the worthiest
    And of þe molde merkede and mesured that tyde,   was St. John, called of Him
    Wirchipede be þou Euaungelist with euer-ilke a wyghte,   who was born in
    Þat he wroghte in this werlde wonnande so wyde. 4   Bethlehem.
Louede be þou lufely lugede in lyghte.
    To life ay in lykynge þat lorde the relyede,
    That in Bedleme was borne of a byrde bryghte.
That barne brynge vs to blysse þare beste es to byde;   8
    To byde in his blysse,
    Thare he es, and his
       Dysciples ilkone.   11
    Whare myrthe may noghte mysse,
    That waye þou vs wysse,
       Euaungelist Ihoñ.   14

(2)

¶ Iohn, as þe gete or germandir gente,   A bright jewel among
    As Iasper þe Iowell of gentill perry,   men, dearly loved of that
So was þou daynte as drowry derely endent   Lord that gave us life.
    In his dedis þat for dule endeynede hym to dye. 18
Þou was lufed of þat lorde þat vs lyfe lente,
Þare was na lyueande lede he lete mare by,
Ne na wyghte in þis werlde with hym̄ þat went,
    And by thi werkes I wate þat þou was worthi.   22

XIX. Saint John. His Birth and Character.

   Wele worthi þou ware,
   For thi werkes ay whare,
    And dedis by-dene.   25
   Now forthir to fare,
   Of thi mekenes mare
    W*ith* mouthe will I mene.   28

(3)

Born in Galilee, of Zebedee and Mary, St. John left his father and his nets and went to Jesus.

¶ In Galylee, graythely gome was þou get,
As Godd of his gudnes graunted þe grace,
Zebede thi fadir, the fude þat the fet,
He fedd the and fosterde, þat faire was of face,   32
Þou was myldeste of mode þat eu*er* maṅ mett,
Thi modir highte Mary, swylk menesyng meṅ mase.
The seet scho aste for hir son*n*es myght hir thynk wele sett,
And of thaire syttynge for-sothe hafe sere solace.   36
   Solace was it to þe,
   The pereles of pousté
    Called the full styll.   39
   Þou forsuke thi fadir fre,
   Schipe and nett of þe see,
    And went hym vntill.   42

(4)

His mother and all his worldly goods he abandoned to follow his Lord.

¶ Thi modir, thi mobles, all man*er* of thyng,
Þat any maṅ in his mynde aftir myghte mene,
Of all þe welthe & þe wanes thou hade in kepynge,   45
To cayre w*ith* þat cum*l*y thou keste the full clene.
W*ith* þat lorde for to lende was thi lykynge,
And for his lufe all lythes lefte thou by-dene.   48
   By-dene lefte þou it all,
   Þat was thyne in-with walle,
    The werlde þou for-suke.   51

[leaf 231, bk.]

   Thare-by sett thou bot smalle
   When thou coṁ to his calle,
    As witnese the buke.   54

XIV. *Saint John. He was Christ's Cousin and Favourite.*

(5)

¶ Thou was witty and wyse, thi werkes vn-wylde,
  Þou werede the fro wyrkynges, wrechid þat ware,
Þou was methe & meke as mayden for mylde,
  Thi mynde moued þou[1] fro myse one ilke a manere, 58
Thou was faire and fayntles, with na fylthe filede,
  Ne with na fandyng thi flesche defoulede with na fere,
For-thi was þou chosen chaste as a child,
  Oure cheftane he chose the, vnchangide of chere. 62
    Thi chere was full chaste
    Fro werkes all waste,
      Noghte assentand to syn. 65
    Full gude was thi gaste,
    Na filthe had defaste
      The verray virgyn. 68

He was wise and meek and pure and good

(6)

¶ Thow was sybbe oure saueoure, hir syster sone,
  Whas semely sydis saluede oure sare,
Þat was þe byrde so bryghte, with birdyn ȝode bun,
  And þe barne alþir-beste of body scho bare. 72
Bathe frenchipe and faythe to frayste it bese fun,
  In þat frely fude to folowe his fare,
For-thi with þat worthi, Iohn, wald þou wonn,
  And with hym walke whate way, þat his will ware. 76
    Ware his will was to wende,
    Or hym lyked to lende,
      Bathe myldely and still, 79
    Þou helde þe ay with þat hende,
    And ferde forthe with thi frende,
      And wroghte at his wyll. 82

Akin after the flesh to the Saviour. His faithful follower in all things.

(7)

¶ Thou was preué with þat prynce in euer-ilk a place;
  To the he publischede þe poyntis of his preuaté,
Firste when þat frely transfegurede his face,
  To a fone of his folke, a ferly to see. 86

In the Transfiguration.

[1] *For* þe.

XIV. Saint John. Care of Christ's Mother. He is tortured.

and at the Supper special grace was shewn to him.

Seþen at the supere, thorghe souerayne grace,
    Many selcouthe syghte schewede he to þe.
For þou was trayste and trewe, and folowede his trace,
    And tuke at his techyng, þat faythfull es and free. 90
        Free fro thralle vs to brynge,
        Heghe one rude walde he hynge,
        So lawe wald he lende. 93
        And þou, his derlyng,
        His modir in kepyng,
        To þe he be-kende. 96

(8)

St. John kept the holy mother with care and duty.

¶ Thou was bouxsom and bayne, hir body to tent,
    And to his byddyng bowand to blysse þat vs broghte,
Thou seruede þat semly till hir sone sent
    Aftir hir hym-selfen; and sythen þou soghte, 100

After her departure, [leaf 232.] he went into Asia, and preached.

In-to Asye þe way warly thou went,
    Thare worthyly werkes of wirchipe þou wroghte,
Prechide appertely the puple repent; 103
    Thorghe prikkynge of penance fra paynes þou thaym broghte;
        Þou broghte thaym to blysse
        Thorowe mendynge of mysse;
        Gret kirkes þou made. 107
        Þe Emperoure of þis
        Was warre, as I wysse,
        And hatrede he hade. 110

(9)

Domitian, the heathen emperor, had him seized,

¶ Domycyane, þat deuyls lymme, dedeyned at þi dede
    And demyd the, for thi doynge, with dule for to dye,
With tyrauntez he tuk the als theefe in þat thede; 113
    Thay toylede the by-twene thaym, and threted the thraly.
Thase licherouse lurdans, laytheste in lede,
    To PorteLatyn thase laddes the ledden full laythely;
Thane the boustoure balde, with barett he bedde
    That thay thi body suld bare, with bale for to bye. 118

XIV. *Saint John. He is banished, but returns to Ephesus.*

  To by was þou made bare,
  And done in a tonñ thare,
   With oyle wellande hate.   121   *and boiled in oil; then laid*
  Seþeñ wald þay noghte spare;
  Þay sett the full sare   *on an iron plate.*
   One ane yreñ plate.   124

(10)

Of aƚƚ þe dedes þay couthe doo, þat derfe ware & diƚƚ,   *But no tortures could*
 Thou dyede noghte, for thaire dede dide no dere vn-to the; *hurt him.*
Foulely foullede þay thi flesche, ȝit felid þou nane iƚƚe,
 For-thi þi fameñ the flemede owte of cuntre.   128   *Therefore he was banished*
Þan to Pathmos, a place, passede þou vn-tyƚƚ,   *to Patmos, where he*
 The Apocalips in that place, with a peñ free   *wrote the Apocalypse.*
Wysely þou wrate it, with witt and with wiƚƚ;
 And for thi werke þou ware worthi wirchipede to be.   132
  To be wirchiped with myghte,
  Þou ware worthi fuƚƚ ryghte
   In euer-ilk a place.   135
  Thou was witnes of lyghte,
  That wysses euer-ilk a wyghte
   Thi name es Goddes grace.   138

(11)

Grete grace was þe gyffeñ & grauntede also,
 Thurghe His gudnes, þat gyfes vs aƚƚ gyftes of mayne :
Whils þou suggeourned in þat suyle, Domycyane, thi foo,   *But Domitian being slain,*
 At a semle, þat segge, in certayne was slayne.   142
Þan þou gysed the gerne, and gafe þe to goo
 Till Ephesyñ graythely þe gates þat ware gayne.   *St. John returned to*
Feele folke ware thi frendes þare þou ferde froo,   *Ephesus, where he was*
 And for to frayste of thi fare, þe toþer ware fayne.   146   *joyfully received.*
  Fayne ware þe folke free,
  And come rynnande to the,
   And hailsed the hame.   149
  And saide þus vn-to the,
  'Blissede ay mote he be,
   Þat commes in Goddes name!'   152

102 XIV. *Saint John. The Miracles he works.*

(12)

[leaf 232, bk.] Thane was Drucyane dede, thi derlynge so dere,
He raised
Drucyane And sulde to delfynge be done, dredles, þat daye,
to life.
　　　Bot þou bade thayme habyde, and sett down þe bere,
　　　　Then blyssede þe body, bare þare it laye. 156
　　　Scho sett hir vp softely with a blythe chere,
　　　　Als scho hade slepede, it semede, sothe for to saye;
Many folk Þay hade wondir of þat wyghte, þe wyes þat þere ware,
followed
St. John.　And all wirchipede thi werke, þat wente by þe waye. 160
　　　　　By þe way þay þat went,
　　　　　Þay lefte landis and rent,
　　　　　　With the for to wende; 163
　　　　　To no thyng tuke þay tent,
　　　　　And sone sum of thaym repent,
　　　　　　By fondyng of þe fende. 166

(13)

He turned Þay ware cumbyrde in couetyse, þe caytefs had care,
sticks into
gold, and 　For þaire knaues ware cledde in clethyng full clene,
made pre-
cious stones. And þay hade no thyng in hande as þay had hadde are,
　　　　And ware noghte halden so myghty as þay had are bene;
　　　For-thi wroghte þou þaire will: of wandes þat ware, 171
　　　　Thow made golde full gude, and gafe þam, I wene;
　　　Smale stanes of þe see, saynede þou þare, 173
　　　　And þay warre saphirs; for-sothe was nane swylke sene.
　　　　　Sene swylke was þare none,
　　　　　For fyne precyouse stone.
　　　　　　The wandes when þou badde, 177
　　　　　Þay ware golde ylkone:
　　　　　Þou gafe thaym welthe mare wone
　　　　　　Þan þay euer hadde. 180

(14)

He raised a When þay had welthe more wane þan þay euer bewanne,
child to life,
　　　　Þay wente home: by þe waye, vnwysely þay wroghte.
　　　A ȝonge barne in þat burghe was dede ryghte thane;
　　　　Þat ilke body þat hym bare, to bale scho was broghte. 184

XIV. *Saint John. Poison does not hurt him.*

His modir come murnande, with hir many mane:
To the made thay thayre mane, mele myghte thay noghte;
And for thay grett so grysely, to grete þou bygane;
 To Godd, of his gudnes, seþen þou besoghte;   188
  Þou besoghte Godd of myghte;
  Þan þe childe rase vpe-ryghte,
   And tolde þam full euen   191   *who testified against the lovers of gold.*
  Þat lett by þi lare lyghte,
  And couetede þe golde bryghte,
   How þay hadd loste heuen.   194

(15)

Than thay wepede and weryede þaire werke and þaire wyll, *The gold-*
 Þat þay, for welthe of þe werlde, sulde wende vn-to woo; *lovers did penance, and*
Thow said, 'will ȝe suffire sothely and still *the gold and precious*
 Seuen dayes penance?' and sonne said thay 300.   198 *stones turned back again.*
Thay tuke at thi techynge, and traysted þar-tyll;
 Þay had for-thynkyng in thoghte, þat þay it fledde froo.
Þe precyouse stones semly to see appon syll,
 And þe golde in thaire kynde, a-gayne gun þay goo. 202
  Thay go agayne in degre   [leaf 233.]
  As þaire kynde was to bee,
   Stones as þay ware.   205
  The golde turnede to wandis free;
  Þan þat syghte fra thay see,
   Myse didd þay na mare.   208

(16)

In þat cuntre was a clerke knawen and kende, *A cunning*
 Þay callede hym Craton þe cunande, thurghe-owte clergy, *clerk called Craton op-*
All þe lande and þat lede þat he gun in lende, *posed St. John, and*
 With his lawes and his lare warre þay ledd by;   212 *tried to poison him.*
Þat philosophir, all þe folke faste he defende
 That thay suld noghte in thi faythe, Iohn, þam affy.
Þus merrede he þe men, þaire mysse for to mende,
 And thurghe mawmetis he made mon a maystry.   216

XIV. Saint John. He bids folk love others as themselves.

   Thurgh thaym, the he soghte;
   For the, Iohn, forsothe he wroghte,
    A puysoñ to profe the.   219
   He saide, as he thoghte,
   'If it noyede the noghte,
    Þañ walde he lufe the.'   222

(17)

The poison slew two prisoners, but St. John restored them, and drank the cup without harm.

Bot þat puysoñ to profe, that prouddeste in palle,
 Profirde it two presoners, was puneschede in pyne,
Als faste als þay felyd it, downe dede guñ þay falle,
 So was it fell for to frayste, þe fylthe was so fyne.   226
Bot þou sanede thaym̄ alsone, seande thaym alle,
 And saynede þe coppe owtely, and suppede it off syne;
Thow hade no harme: þat be-helde þat hendeste in hall,
 And to the hally þay heledide, bathe he and his hyne.
   His hyne holly, and he,
   Trewely trowede þare to þe,
    Be-come þare thi brothire.   233
   Þou said to þat menȝe,
   'Luke þat ȝe lufande be,
    Ilkone to oþer.'   236

(18)

He preacht brotherly love and charity.

Thou bade thaym be free to frayste in þaire fare,
 Faythefull and frendely till euerilk a fere,
'What may þis mene' quod these meñ, 'mone it vs mare;
 We hafe no mencyoñ ne mynde of þis matere.'   240
'It es þe commandement of Criste, þat I ȝow declare,
 To kepe it be connande all mankynde clere,
Luke ȝe releue ilke a lede þat lykes ȝoure lare,
 To lufe ilk mañ as ȝoure selfe: this lessoñ ȝe lere.'   244
   To lere nowe þis ryghte,
   Gret Godd of his myghte
    Graunte ȝow þe grace!   247
   And Ihesu, þat worthi wyghte,
   Helpe vs all to þat lyghte
    For to see his face!   250

XIV. *Saint John. He is taken to Heaven.*

(19)

Wyse men and witty, þat of thi werkes wyste,
    Weled the for wo[r]thi wirchipe to welde;   252
To be þaire beschope, blithely þay bedde the so blyste,
    For þou myghte, in thaire bale, beste be thaire belde;
Thay menskede the with manhede, with mytir vn-myste,
    And folowed thi fare freely in frythe and in felde.   256
Thus thow lyffede in the lande whils oure Lorde lyste,
    And when hym lykede, he laghte the, thi gaste þou gun
        hym ȝelde.
        For to ȝelde the thi mede,
        In heuen for thi gude dede,
           When þou heþen paste,   261
        He was redy, we rede.
        To þat lyghte he vs lede,
           Þat euer-more sall laste!   Amen!   264
           Explicit.

Marginalia: The wise men of Ephesus desired St. John to be [leaf 233 bk.] their bishop. — In God's own time, He took St. John to Heaven. — May He light us there too!

[Follows, the prose treatise that begins, 'Praying [MS. Prayng] is a gracyous gyfte of owre lorde godd,' &c.]

XV. EARTH UPON EARTH.

[In a later hand, on leaf 279.]
Memento, Homo, Quod Cinis Es, Et in cinerem Reuerteris[1].
(Five verses of 4: *a a a a*.)

(1)

Limus.
Man of earth
or clay.

*Homo
primus.*

Erthe owte of erthe es wondirly wroghte;
Erthe hase getyn one erthe a dignyte of noghte;
Erthe appon erthe hase sett alle his thoghte,
How þat erthe appon erthe may be heghe broghte.   4

(2)

Sordens.

[lf. 279 bk.]

Erthe appon erthe wolde be a kynge;
Bot howe þat erthe to erthe sall, thynkis he no thynge.
When erthe bredis erthe, and his rentis home brynge[2],
Thane schalle erthe of erthe hafe full harde partynge.   8

(3)

*Mutare
nequimus.*
gets castles
and property,
and says they
are his, and
Vnde

Erthe appon erthe wynnys castells and towrrys;
Thus saise erthe vn-to erthe, 'this es alle owrris;'
When erthe appon erthe hase bigged vp his bowrris,
Than schalle erthe for erthe suffire scharpe stowrrys.   12

(4)

Superbimus.
goes glittering
like gold.

Terram
But he must

Erthe gose appon erthe, as golde appon golde;
He that gose appon erthe gleterande as golde,
Lyke als erthe neuer-more goo to erthe scholde,
And ȝitt schall erthe vn-to erthe ȝa rathere þan he wolde.   16

(5)

turn to earth
again; and
send out
Terra

Redimus.
a foul stink.

Now why þat erthe luffis erthe, wondire me thynke,
Or why þat erthe for erthe scholde oþer swete or swynke
For when þat erthe appon erthe es broghte with-in brynnke;
Thane schalle erthe of erthe hafe a foulle stynke.   20

Mors Soluit Omnia.

[1]. Against the title in the margin is written:—'Perce mihi domine nichil enim sunt dies mei: quid est homo . . . .'
[2] This line is repeated on the leaf's back, with *rentys* for *rentis*.

XVI. SERVE AND LOVE CHRIST.

Robert Thornton's MS. (cir. 1440).

(*Twenty alternates: ab ab. Two lines written as one.*)

(1)

Þ I Ioy be, ilke a dele,   [leaf 222.]
   To *ser*ue thi Godd' to paye,   Rejoice in serving God.
For all this worldes wele
   Þou sese it wytes a-waye.   4
Thow fande, his lufe to fele   Try to feel His love.
   Þat laste will *with* the aye,
And þan þi care sall kele
   And pyne *tur*ne the to playe,   8

(2)

In Criste þou caste thi thoghte,   Hate wrath and pride.
   Hate all wrethe and pryde,
And thynke þat he þe boghte
   With woundis depe and wyde   12
Whem þou selfe hase soghte,
   Full wele the sall be-tyde;
Of reches, rekke þou noghte   Care not for riches.
   Fra helle þat he the hyde.   16

(3)

Thay *tur*ne þair*e* day to nyghte
   Þat lufes þis erthely syñ,
And slayne ere in þat fyghte
   Þare we oure lyfe sall wyñ.   20
For þat þay lufe vnryghte   Lovers of wrong shall sit in Hell.
   And þare-of kane noghte blyñ;
Þay lose þe lande of lyghte
   And hellë sittis with-in.   24

XVI. *Serve and Love Christ.*

(4)

<small>Lift up your heart to Christ.</small>

Thou do als I þe rede,
   Lyftande vpe thi herte,
And say tilt hym was ded,
   Criste! my hele þou Arte!   28

<small>Sin weighs you down.</small>

Syn synkës ay as lede,
   And ferrë falles fra qwerte;
For-þi stabill thi stede;
   Þare smyttynge may noghte smerte.   32

(5)

<small>Love your King, Christ,</small>

Lere to lufe thi kynge,
   Whas lufe euer-more will laste;
Haue hym in thi¹ thynkynge,
   And feste his lufe sa faste,   36
That for nane² erthely thynge
   Na qwayntyse may it caste.
Thi sange [be² his, for t]hi swetynge
   He will be at þe laste.   40

(6)

<small>and seek solace in Him.</small>

In Criste² conayte thi solace;
   His lufë chaunge thi chere;
With Ioy þou take his grace,
   And syghe to sytt hym nere.   44
Euer sekande his face,
   Þou make þi saulë clere³;
He ordaynes hye thi place,
   If þou þis lyfe will lere.   48

(7)

<small>Keep His Ten Commandments.</small>

Thou kepe his byddynges ten;
   Halde the fra dedly syn;
Forsake þe Ioy of men,
   Þat þou his lufe may wyn.   52

---

¹ MS. 'in thi thy thynkynge.'   ² MS. rubbed.
³ *may* crossed out before *make* in MS.

XVI. *Serve and Love Christ.*

Thi herte, of hym̄ sałł bryn̄;
ʒour lufe sałł neuer twyn̄;
Langynge he wiłł þe len̄,   *He will make*
    To won̄ heuen̄ with-in.   56 *Heaven.*

        (8)

Thow thynke of his mekenes
   How pure þat he was borne;
Be-halde his bludy flesche   *Behold His*
   His heide pungede with thorne.   60 *with thorns,*
Þi lufe, þat it noghte lesse,
   He sauede þe, for-lorne,
To serue hym in swetnes
   For ałł þat hafe we sworne.   64

        (9)

Festyn̄ þi herte to flee   *Flee from*
   Ałł þis werldes care,   *this world's*
That þou in ryste may be   *cares.*
   Þou salfe þi saulës sare.   68
His lufe, take it to þe   *Take Christ's*
   And lufe hym mare & mare,   *love to you,*
His face þat þou may see
   When þou sałł heþen̄ fare.   72

       (10)

If þou be in fandynge,
   Of lufe þou has grete nede,   *which you*
To stedde þe in stabillynge   *so need.*
   And gyffe þe grace to spede.   76
Thow duełł ay with þi kynge,   *Feed ever in*
   And in his lufe þe fede,   *Christ's love.*
For littiłł I hafe cunnynge
   To tełł of his fairhede.   80

XVI. *Serve and Love Christ.*

(11)

¶ Bot lufe hym at thi myghte
 Whilis þou ert lyfande here,
And luke vpe to þat syghte
 Þat mon be the so dere.   84
Say till hym day and nyghte,
 'When may I neghe þe nere?
Rayse me vpe to þe, ryghte,
 Thi melodye to here.'   88

(12)

In that lyfe þe stedde,
 Þat þou be ay lufande,
And gyffe hym lufe to wedde,
 Þat þou with hym will stande. 92
Ioy in thi breste es bredde
 When þou erte hym lufande;
Thi saule þan hase he fedde,
 In swete lufe ay brennande.   96

(13)

¶ All vanytese for-sake,
 If þou his lufe will fele;
Thi herte þou hym by-take;
 He cane it kepe full wele.   100
Thi myrthe na man may make
 Of Godd' es ilke a dele.
Thi thoghte, late it noghte qwake;
 Thi lufe, late it noghte kele. 104

(14)

¶ Of syn, þe bitternes,
 Thow flee ay faste þare fraa;
This werldes wikkednes,
 Luke it noghte with þe gaa.   108

XVI. *Serve and Love Christ.*

This erthely besynes,
   Þat hase men wirkede waa;
Thi lufe it will make lesse,
   If þou it to þe taa.   112

(15)

¶ All we lufe som thynge,
   Þat knawynge hase of skyll,
And hafe þare in lykynge,
   When it may com vs till.   116
For-thi, doo Cristes byddynge,
   And lufe hym als he will,
Whas lufe hase nane endynge,
   And Ioye with-owten ill.   120

(16)

¶ Thay þat lufes fleschly,
   Ere lykenede to þe swyne:
In filthe þan will þay lye,
   Thaire fairehede will þay tyne.   124
Thair lufe partes purely
   And puttede es in pyne;
Swetter es lufe gastely,
   Þat neuer-mare wyll d[yme].   128

(17)

¶ If þou lufe whils þou may,
   The kynge of mageste,
Thi wa wendis a-way.
   Thi hele hyes to þe,   132
Thi nyghte turnes in-to day,
   Thi blysse mon euer be
When þou erte as I say,
   I pray þe thynke one mee.   136

(18)

¶ Our thoghtes sall we sette,
 To-gedire in heuen to duelle,
For þare þe gude er mette,
 Þat Christe haldes fra helle. 140
When we oure synns hafe grett,
 Þe tythandes may we telle,
Þat we fra ferre hase fette
 Þe lufe þat man sall felle. 144

(19)

¶ The werlde, caste it by-hynde,
 And say 'Ihesu, my swete,
Faste in thi lufe me bynde,
 And gyffe me grace to grete, 148
To lufe the, turne my kynde,
 And for to lufe the, I hete
That I thi lufe may fynde,
 Þat will my bales wele bete. 152

(20)

¶ With lufe wounde me with-in,
 And to þi lyghte me lede;
Thow make me clene of syn,
 Þat me thare noghte þe drede. 156
As þou, to saue man-kyn,
 Sufferd þi sydis to blede,
Gyfe me witt to wyn
 The syghte of þe to mede.' 160

(21)

¶ His lufe es [pure] and trewe,
 Who-so hym lufeande ware,
Sen firste þat I it knewe,
 It kepide me fro care. 164

I fand it eu*er* new
   To lere me Goddes lare,
And now thaie me noghte rewe
   þat I haffe sufferde sare.   168

(22)

¶ In lufe thi harte þou heghe,
   And fyghte to felle þe fende;
Thi dayes sall be vndreghe,
                          172

When thi ded neghes neghe,
   And thow sall heþen wende,
Thow sall hym see wit*h* eghe,
   And cum to Criste, thi frende.   176

XVII. [WHAT THUNDER SIGNIFIES IN DIFFERENT MONTHS.]

[*Robert Thornton's MS.* (leaf 50).]

No*tandum*, þat by tokyns off þe Element þat falles In þe moneth, a man schall knawe Plenteth and darke By þe monethes.

In January. Thono*ur* In Ieneuere, sygnyfyes, þat seme ȝere, grette wyndys and grette plentye off cornes, and grette batall also.

In February. Thono*ur* In Feuerȝere, sygnyfyes, þat seme ȝere, þat mony men schall deye, and namlye rychys men.

In March. Thono*ur* In Marche, sygnyfyes, þat seme ȝere, grett wyndes, plentethe off cornes, and grette stryff a-manges þe peple.

In April. Thono*ur* In Auerell, sygnyfyes, þat seme ȝere to be Frutfull & mery, And also grette dede off wekkyde men͡.

In May. Thono*ur* In May, sygnyfyes, that same ȝere, wyckednese of frut; and grette havng*ur* In many place yt tokneysse.

In June. Thono*ur* In Iune, sygnyfyes, þat same ȝere, woddyse þat or wattyr with dent of wynde schall falle; & grette wodnese of woluese & lyons þat ȝere schall be.

In July. Thono*ur* In Iuly, sygnyfyes, þat same ȝere, a gode ȝer; and grete synner schalle spytt.

[leaf 50 bk.] In October. Thono*ur*[1] In octobyr, sygnyfyes, þat same ȝere, grete wyndys & grete skantenesse of cornnys, & lytyll frowytese on trees.

In November. Thono*ur* In nouembyr, sygnyfyes, þat same ȝere, þat all thynges sall be frowtfull & mery, & also plentethe of cornne.

In December. Thono*ur* In Desembyr, sygnyfyes, þat same ȝere, plentethe of cornes, and mekyll whete and pesse, And reste amanges þe peple of þat rewme þer yt falles In.

[1] The upper portion of the original f. 50-50 bk. is lost, hence the signification of thunder in August and September is missing.

[Leaf 51 a. Blank.]

XVIII.
[THE LAMENTATION OF A DYING SINNER.]

Lamentacio Peccatoris.

(1)

Aɫɫ crystyn men þat wawkes me bye,
  Be-hold & see þis dulfuɫ seyght!   *[leaf 51 bk.]*
I beyd nothere to kawɫ nor to crye,   *Let all Christians look on me!*
  I am so dampyd, a wofuɫ weyght.   4   *I am damned.*

(2)

Tayk heyd of me, both kyng & kneyt,
  & mend yow heyr qwylles ȝe have space;   *Mend your ways while you have time!*
Fore qwen ȝe haue lost euer-lastyng leght,
  Fro mercy be gone, ȝe gayt no grace.   8

(3)

Qwen I was ȝowyng, es now er ȝe,
  Þan beyd I neuer a fayrere lyfe:
I spent my ȝerys in vanite,   *I wasted my life, and I*
  In vane glory & in stryfe.   12

(4)

I had no hape, qwylles I was heyre,
  To ryes & me repent;
Now am I broght apon a beyre:
  Itt ys to lett, for I am schentt.   16   *am ruind.*

(5)

Gret othes, to me þa war fuɫ ryfe,   *I sware*
  I had no grace for to a-mende;
I sparyd neuer noder madyn ne wyfe,   *and whored,*
  & þat hase browght me to þis ende;   20

XVIII. *The Lamentation of a Dying Sinner.*

(6)

<small>stuft, and</small>

In lecheri I led my lyfe:
Qwen I had God & gud at Wyll,
I sclew my self wi*th*-out a knyfe;
In glotonye I toyk my fyll.   24

(7)

<small>lazied.</small>

<small>Now it is 'Had I but known my end!'</small>

In sclewyth I lay, & sclepyd styll;
I was desauyd throw a tryst;
Þis dredful ded I druwe my tyll,
And all ys tornyd to adywyst.   28

(8)

<small>Rest not in your sin.</small>
<small>¹ This line is repeated in the MS.</small>

'Add I wyst' yt wyll not bee;
I wot I mune neu*er* more thweyn,
For*e* hym þat dyed for ȝow & me,
Ryes, & rest not i*n* ȝowr synn!¹   32

(9)

<small>[leaf 51 bk., col. 2.]</small>

<small>I had no God but money.</small>

¶ Qwen I was lapyd in synnys seyr*e*,
Sore to yow I mayk my mone,
Þ*er* meght me help no gud prayer;
I had no God, bot gud a-lone.   36

(10)

<small>I was as young (?) blithe as a bird.</small>
<small>Now I suffer.</small>

¶ Qwen I was ȝown, & in my flowres,
I was as blythe as byrd on breyr;
Þat garrys me suffer þese scherp schoris,
And by þis bargan wond*er* deyr*e*.   40

(11)

<small>Woe to them</small>

<small>who will not take warning by me!</small>

¶ Woo to þes, wer-eu*er* þa bee,
That hase þ*er* v inwytt*es* to wyll,
Þat wyl not now tayk tent to me,
& knawe þe gud byfor þe yll.   44

XVIII. *The Lamentation of a Dying Sinner.*

(12)

¶ Pure, for fawt, ȝe lat not spyll,
    For & ȝe do, ȝowr ded ys deght;
The lust of ȝowr fleych wyl neuer ful-fyll;
    By-war in luste; fer not at ȝe lyght.   48

(13)

¶ In deligat metys I had gret delytt,   *I ate and drank:*
    So had I wyne on-to my pay;
Þat garres þes wormes on me to byt,   *now dragons bite me.*
    And euer þer sang ys 'wyllossay!'   52

(14)

¶ I meght not fast, nor I wold not pray;   *I wouldn't pray.*
    I thoyt to a mendyd in my egge[1];   [1 age.]
I draue euer of, fro day to day,
    And now am I lokyk[2] in a kage.   56   [2 locked.]

(15)

¶ The kage, yt be on byrnyng fyere,   *Now I am in the fire*
    Þat I am ordand in to dwell:
Thys haue þa gyuyn me to my hyere,
    Euer to last in þe panes of hell.   60   *of Hell,*

(16)

¶ Thus am I feterd with fendys so fell,   *bound by fiends like beasts in a stall.*
    As qwo bynd besse in-to a stall:
Þer ys no tong, my woo kan tell;
    By-war, gud serys, of syche a fall!   64   *Take warning by me!*

(17)

¶ Gentyll brother, haue in mynd,   [leaf 52.]
    Hyen qwen þou schall weynd away;   *Brother, be*
To þi awyn sall, be neuer onkynd,   *not unkind to your soul!*
    Remember þat, bothe nyght & day!   68

XVIII. *The Lamentation of a Dying Sinner.*

(18)

Pray Christ to save you

¶ Full derly to hym þat ȝe pray,
To hym þat was don a-pon a tre,

on Doomsday!

To safe ȝowr sallis on dowymysday.
Qwen all sall*es*, sauyd mon be. 72

(19)

Then, no man can

¶ Than may þ*er*, na *ler*nyd men for ȝow mute,
No iustys, nor no man of lawe,
For, & þ^a [do], þ^a be no buyt,

help you.

Þ*er* charter wyll not preyf worthe a hawe. 76

(20)

¶ Thus eu*er*y Man, ȝe tayk gud tent,
Eu*er*y Man in hys de-gre!
Me thynk I heyr a horn blowe:

Christian men, be warned by me

All crystyn men, be war by me! 80

Explicit lamentacio.

XIX.

[*Robert Thornton's MS.*, leaf 176, col. 2.]

A charme for þe tethe werke.

Say þe charme thris, to it be sayd ix tymes,
And ay thris at a charemynge.

---

(1)

I conjoure the, laythely beste, wi*th* þat ilke spere   *I conjure you, loathsome beast,*
Þ*at* Longyous in his hande ga*n* bere,
And also wi*th* ane hatte of thorne
Þ*at* one my Lordis hede was borne,   4
Wi*th* alle þe wordis mare & lesse,
Wi*th* þe Office of þe Messe,   *by the Mass, by Christ, Our Lady, St.*
Wi*th* my Lorde and his xij postills,   *Margaret and*
Wi*th* oure Lady and hir x Maydenys,   8 *St. Katherine,*
[With] Saynt Marg[a]rete þe quene,
Saynt Kat*er*in þe haly virgyne,
ix tymes Goddis forbott, þou wikkyde worme,
Þat eu*er* þou make any rystynge;   12
Bot awaye mote þou wende,   *to go away to earth.*
To þe erde and þe stane!   14

(2)

Thre gude breþ*er* are ȝe;   *You are 3 good brothers.*
Gud gatis gange ȝe!
haly thynges, seke ȝe;   *Seek holy things.*
he says 'will ȝe telle me?'   18
he sais 'blissede Lorde, mot ȝe be!
It may neu*er* gety*n* be,

XIX. *Charm for the Toothache.*

Lorde, bot ȝour willis be.'
Settis douṅ appoṅ ȝour knee,   22
Gretly athe suere ȝe me,
By Mary modir mylke so fre.   24
   There es no maṅ þat euer hase nede,
ȝe schaft hym charme, & aske no mede;
And here saft I lere it the:—
As þe Iewis wondide me,   28
Þay wende to wonde me fra þe grounde;
I helyd my selfe, bathe hale & sounde.
Ga to þe cragge of Olyuete;
Take oyle de bayes, þat es so swete;   32
And thris abowte this worme ȝe strayke;
This bethe þe worme þat schotte noghte,
Ne kankire noghte, ne falowe noghte,
And als clere hale fra þe grounde   36
Als Ihesu dyde with his faire wondis.
Þe Fadir, & þe Soṅ, & þe Haly Gaste.
And Goddis forbott, þou wikkyde worme,
Þat euer þou make any ris[t]ynge or any sugorne![1] 40
Bot awaye mote þou wende,
To þe erth and þe stane!   42

Marginal notes: *Kneel down and swear to me.* — *I, Christ, will tell you the charm.* — *Go to the Mount of Olives, get oil of bays, put it thrice round the worm,* — *and bid it not stay, but go to earth.*

[1] or any sugorne *interlined*.

GLOSSARY.

A.

a, *adj.* one, 3/18, 20, 16/10.
abowte-gangande, *prp.* surrounding, 49/6.
adywyst, *sb.* had-I-known (how it would have turned out), after-regret, 116/28; add I wyst, 116/29.
affy, *vb. inf.* trust, 103/214.
agaynestande, *vb. inf.* withstand, 18/21.
aghte, *vb.* 3 *sg. pr.* ought, 64/30, 74/400.
alegeance, *sb.* alleviation, relief, 9/5, 29/29.
alkyn, *adj.* all kinds of, all, 5/14, 7/30, 8/25.
als-swa, *adv.* also, 7/15.
al-þer-fyrste, *adv.* first of all, 42/10.
alpire-beste, *adj.* best of all, 32/36.
al-þir-flrste, *adj.* first of all, 54/24.
al-þir-myghtyeste, *adj.* mightiest of all, 32/36.
alpirwyseste, *adj.* wisest of all, 32/36.
ambynowre, *sb.* almoner, 56/34.
anehede, *sb.* unity, 47/20, 21, 63/8.
anence, *prep.* anent, concerning, 3/4, 5/11.
anlypy, *adj.* single, 14/14.
anouren, *vb.* 3 *pl. pr.* honour, 23/13.
anoye, *sb.* annoyance, 13/30.
anykyn, *adj.* any kind of, 33/6.
aperte, *adv.* openly, 24/21; in apperte, 23/33; apertely, 47/28; appertly, 40/11.
appropirde, *vb. pp.* attributed, 21/28, 28/32, 33, 34, 48/5.
are, *adv.* before, 7/31.
arely, *adv.* early, 13/7, 60/16.
assethe, *sb.* satisfaction, 7/1.
assoylede, *vb. pp.* absolved, 6/36.
aste, *vb.* 3 *sg. pt.* asked, 98/35.
at, *conj.* that, 31/35, 32/10; *rel. pron.* which, 13/23, 24, 18/12, 13.
at, *prep.* to, 8/29, 26/22, 36/34.
athes, *sb. pl.* oaths, 7/3.
aughte, *sb.* property, possessions, 89/49.
aughten, *adj.* eighth, 6/18, 67/153
aughtened, 29/20.
autyr, *sb.* alter, 8/26.
auauntez, *vb.* 3 *sg. pr.* boasts, vaunts, 24/12.
auauntynge, *sb.* vaunting, 12/18.
avowtry, *sb.* adultery, 14/17.
avysede, *adj.* devised, contrived, 21/9.
awe, *vb.* 3 *sg. pr.* ought, 3/26, 5/10, 8/28; 3 *pl. pr.* 2/1.
awen, *adj.* own, 1/8, 5/1.
ayere, *sb.* air, 1/7.
ayers, *sb. pl.* hairs, 32/30.
aysell, *sb.* vinegar, 70/252.

B.

barett, *sb.* sorrow, pain, 100/117.
barne-tyme, *sb.* brood of children, 61/15.
bathere, *adj.* of both, 9/15.
bawndon, *sb.* control, power, 76/27.
baylyes, *sb. pl.* bailiffs, 55/14.
bayne, *adj.* prompt, ready, 100/97.
bed, *vb.* 3 *pl. pt.* offered, 70/250.
bedde, *vb.* 3 *pl. pt.* beseeched, 105/253.
bede, *sb.* prayer, 77/14.
bedyn, *vb. pp.* bidden, 3/2.
bekende, *vb.* 3 *sg. pt.* consigned, 100/96.
belde, *sb.* comfort, strength, 105/254.
bemes, *sb. pl.* trumpets, 89/37.
benyson, *sb.* blessing, 31/21.
bese, *vb.* 3 *sg. pr.* is, 91/94, 99/73.
besse, *sb. pl.* beasts, 117/62.
besy, *adj.* anxious, careful, 17/16.
besynes, *sb.* trouble, 38/19.
betakynde, *vb. pp.* betokened, 38/18.
bete, *vb. imp.* remedy, 81/71; *inf.* 112/152.
beteche, *vb.* 1 *sg. pr.* commend, 77/10.
bethe, *vb.* 3 *sg. subj.* foments, 120/34.
beyd, *vb.* 1 *sg. pr.* desire, crave, 115/3; 1 *sg. pt.* 115/10.

·122   *Glossary.*

bigged, *vb. pp.* built, 106/11.
birdyn, *sb.* burden, child, 99/71.
bla, *adj.* livid, 94/58.
ble, *sb.* complexion, colour, 91/87;
    blee, 94/59.
blyn, *vb.inf.* cease, 74/415; blynnes,
    3 *sg. pr.* 2/3, 10/30.
blyschede, *pp. adj.* worthy to be
    blessed, 41/31.
bodyly, *adv.* in the body, 4/12.
bollenynge, *sb.* swelling, 12/32.
bot if, *conj.* unless, 6/36, 8/31.
boustoure, *sb.* ruffian, tyrant,
    100/117.
bouxome, *adj.* obedient, 6/2, 54/36
bouxomnes, *sb.* obedience, 54/30.
bown, *adj.* ready, prepared, 70/253,
    90/65.
brace, *vb. inf.* embrace, 91/92.
braste, *vb.* 3 *sg. pt.* burst, 44/23.
brede, *vb. pp.* bred, 14/8.
brennande, *vb. prp.* burning,
    110/96.
bristes, *vb.* 3 *sg. pr.* bursts, 71/294.
brwke, *vb.* 1 *pl. pr.* enjoy the use of,
    profit by, 90/80.
brynnynge, *sb.* burning, 23/31.
bryste, *vb. inf.* burst, 59/25.
bufettes, *sb. pl.* blows, 68/202;
    bofetes, 42/36.
bun, *adj.* 99/71, *v.* bown.
burde, *vb.* 3 *sg. pt.* fell to, behoved,
    94/64, 66.
buse, *vb.* 3 *sg. pr.* behoves, 89/38;
    bude, 3 *sg. pt.* 93/41.
bute, *sb.* remedy, 95/97; buyt,
    118/75.
by, *vb. inf.* buy, redeem, 29/12,
    36/3.
by-dene, *adv.* at once, 98/48.
byhouely, *adj.* helpful, needful, 5/21.
by-leue, *sb.* belief, 52/29, 30.
byrde, *sb.* woman, lady, maiden,
    97/7, 99/71.
byse, *sb.* sort of fine stuff, 67/147.

C.

carpyng, *sb.* uttering, speaking, 7/35.
cayre, *vb. inf.* go, 98/46.
caytefly, *adv.* wretchedly, 40/19.
caytifede, *adj.* made captive,
    wretched, 38/28.
chasty, *vb. inf.* chastise, correct,
    10/1, 22/26; chastied, *pp.* 22/25.
chaufe, *vb.* 3 *sg. pr.* make warm,
    81/53.
chese, *vb. inf.* choose, 11/20, 29/36.
clergy, *sb.* clergydom, 103/210.

clethe, *vb. inf.* clothe, 9/27, 22/20;
    clede, 3 *pl. pt.* 69/222.
collacyone, *sb.* discourse, 23/26.
comforthe, *sb.* comfort, 55/20.
comfurthe, *vb. inf.* comfort, 55/2.
communers, *sb.* partakers, 1/11.
comonynge, *sb.* communion, 3/22.
comouns, *vb.* 3 *pl. pr.* commune,
    3/24.
complyn, *sb.* last service of the day,
    45/29.
conabilly, *adv.* suitably, 19/13.
conande, *adj.* cunning, skilful,
    51/13.
conandely, *adv.* thoroughly, 14/33;
    cunnandely, 14/35.
conaundenes, *sb.* skill, wisdom,
    knowledge, 13/21.
conclude, *vb. inf.* confute, 90/67.
contekes, *sb. pl.* contests, 25/4.
contende, *vb. pp.* contained, 81/29,
    38/12.
cop(p)e, *sb.* cup, 34/29, 30.
couaite, *vb. inf.* covet, desire, 27/36,
    28/6; couayte, 1 *sg. pr.* 80/41;
    coueites, 3 *sg.pr.* 14/32; couaytes,
    3 *pl. pr.* 27/22.
couetyse, *sb.* covetousness, 6/26.
cufere, *vb. inf.* cover, 90/77.
cun, *vb. inf.* know, 2/35, 14/27; 1
    pl. pr. 10/6; 3 *pl. pr.* 2/28, 33;
    cunnes, 3 *pl. pr.* 14/31.
cunnynge, *sb.* knowledge, wisdom,
    experience, 24/27, 28/22, 29.

D.

dalfe, *vb.* 3 *sg. pt.* delved, 88/1.
darke = darthe, *sb.* dearth, scarcity,
    114/2.
daynte, *adj.* precious, excellent,
    handsome, 97/17.
debonerte, *sb.* gentleness, mildness,
    86/92.
dede, *sb.* death, 3/27, 4/22, 9/5,
    27/18, &c.
dedeyned, *vb. pp.* displeased,
    100/111.
defaste, *vb. pp.* defaced, 99/67.
defaute, *sb.* fault, want, 2/8, 28/30.
defendis, *vb.* 3 *sg. pr.* forbids,
    29/26; defendyde, *pp.* 24/9,
    26/30.
defule, *vb. inf.* trample under foot,
    spurn, 48/26.
delfynge, *sb.* burying, 102/154.
deligat, *adj.* delicate, 117/49.
demynge, *sb.* judging, 61/17.
dent, *sb.* blowing, 114/15.

Glossary. 123

dere, *adj.* dear, 94/64.
dere, *sb.* injury, 101/126.
derfe, *adj.* hard, brutal, 101/125.
dessayues, *vb.* 3 *sg. pr.* deceives, 25/26; dessayfede, *pp.* 18/14.
dill, *adj.* foolish, stupid, 101/125.
dispendis, *vb.* 3 *pl. pr.* spend, 31/17.
doghtyrs, *sb. pl.* daughters, 61/13.
doluen, *pp.* buried, 4/17.
domme, *adj.* dumb, 58/18.
dortoure, *sb.* dormitory, 53/15.
doungen, *vb. pp.* beaten, struck, 43/11.
dowte, *vb. inf.* fear, 23/28.
doynge owte, *sb.* turning out, 8/30.
dredles, *adv.* doubtlessly, 102/154.
drery, *adj.* sad, 85/52.
dreryly, *adv.* miserably, 32/29.
drewrye, *sb.* love, 81/65.
drowry, *sb.* gift, precious thing, 97/17.
druwe, *vb.* 1 *sg. pt.* drew, 116/27.
duellyde, *vb. pp.* remained, 18/35.
dule, *sb.* pain, suffering, grief, sorrow, 73/359, 100/112.
dule, *adj.* foolish, erring, 97/18.
dulful, *adj.* doleful, 115/2.
duse, *vb.* 3 *sg. pr.* does, 29/20; 3 *pl. pr.* 10/8, 13/6, 14/17.
dyme, *vb. inf.* grow dim, 111/128.
dynge, *adj.* worthy, 65/93.
dyspende, *vb.* 1 *pl. pr.* destroy, 23/5; *pp.* dissipated, 17/30.
dyssayued, *vb. pp.* deceived, 37/1.
dysses, *sb.* trouble, 26/7.
dyssessede, *vb. pp.* disseized, dispossessed, 7/5.

E.

efter, *prep.* according to, 5/27, 7/27, 9/10; eftere, 6/4; eftyre, 22/16.
eghe, *sb.* eye, 16/24, 35/24; eghne, *pl.* 53/11.
eke, *vb. inf.* increase, 73/348; ekes, 3 *pl. pr.* 54/18.
elde, *sb.* age, 2/30, 7/27, 8/28, &c.
encheson, *sb.* cause, occasion, 16/13, 27/19, 94/68.
endent, *vb. pp.* fixed in, inlaid, 97/17.
endeynede, *vb.* 3 *sg. pt.* condescended, deigned, 97/18.
enflawmes, *vb.* 3 *sg. pr.* inflames, 59/22.
er(e), *vb.* are, 3 *pl. pr.* 2/21, 5/10, 7/10, 30; erte, 2 *sg. pr.* 17/21.

euen, *adj.* equal, 3/13, 15; euynne, 4/30.
evencristen, *sb.* fellow-Christian, 5/12, 11/6, 12/22, 24/32, &c.
evenhede, *sb.* moderation, 11/29.

F.

faamen, *sb. pl.* foemen, enemies, 84/50, 101/128.
faas, *sb. pl.* foes, 11/25.
faere, *adj. cp.* fewer, 47/16.
falachipe, *sb.* fellowship, 19/23.
fallace, *sb.* deceitfulness, 90/77.
falles, *vb.* 3 *pl. pr.* belong, 2/20, 3/5, 6.
falowe, *vb.* 3 *sg. pr.* fades, 120/35.
fande, *vb. inf.* endeavour, try, tempt, 18/21; *imper.* 12/12, 107/5; fandes, 1 *pl. pr.* 6/7.
fandynge, *sb.* temptation, 11/26, 21/8.
fange, *vb.* 3 *sg. pt.* took, 93/45.
fawt, *sb.* fault, 117/45.
feblesce, *sb.* feebleness, 40/34.
feele, *adj.* many, 101/145.
felaschepe, *sb.* fellowship, 47/12, 13.
felawrede, *sb.* fellowship, 8/23.
fellenes, *sb.* terror, awfulness, 48/7.
fere, *adj.* able to go, strong, healthy, 88/11; ferre, 108/30.
fere, *sb.* companion, wife, mate, 99/60, 104/238.
*ferly, *sb.* wonder, miracle, 99/86.
fermoresse, *sb.* hospital nurse, 57/24.
fermory(e), *sb.* hospital, infirmary, 53/23, 57/25.
fet, *vb.* 3 *sg. pt.* fetched, brought, 98/31; fette, *pp.* 112/143.
feule, *sb.* bird, 14/7; fewle, 88/12.
filede, *vb. pp.* fouled, defiled, 99/59.
flemede, *vb.* 3 *pl. pt.* put to flight, 101/128.
flesche-foldes, *sb. pl.* flesh, 90/56.
flom, *sb.* river, 68/175.
flytynge, *sb.* quarrelling, 13/1.
foghles, *sb. pl.* birds, 65/80.
foly, *vb. inf.* fool, 6/10.
fone, *adj.* few, 31/17, 99/86.
forbeddes, *vb.* 3 *sg. pr.* forbids, 6/10.
forboden, *vb. pp.* forbidden, 5/14, 6/20.
forbott, *sb.* prohibition, 119/11.
forbysen, *sb.* example, 78/361.
force, *sb.* necessity, 47/3.
for-do, *vb. inf.* destroy, 13/2.
forhewe, *vb. inf.* avoid, forsake, 12/4.

124   *Glossary.*

forluke, *sb.* foresight, providence, 4/20.
forme-fadyrs, *sb.* forefathers, 1/17, 21, 4/20.
for-thi, *conj.* therefore, 2/11, 28/29.
for-thi þat, *conj.* because, in order that, 2/4, 35, 14/15.
forthynkynge, *sb.* repentance, 8/18.
for-why, *conj.* because, 55/5.
founde, *vb. inf.* go, hasten, 85/70, 79.
fourtede, *adj.* fourth, 4/27.
fratour, *sb.* refreshment-room of monastery, refectory, 53/14, 56/27.
frayste, *vb. inf.* try, test, experience, learn, ask, 99/73, 101/146, 104/226, 237.
frele, *adj.* frail, 18/21.
frely, *adj.* free, noble, courteous, 99/74, 85.
fremmede, *adj.* not of kin, foreign, 6/11, 61/7.
frenes, *sb.* freedom, liberty, 40/34.
frowytese, *sb. pl.* fruits, 114/20.
frythe, *sb.* forest, 105/256.
fude, *sb.* offspring, person, 89/27, 93/23, 98/31, 99/74.
fule, *sb.* fool, 69/207.
ful(l)e, *adj.* foul, evil, 11/26, 30, 42/34.
fulle, *vb. inf.* foul, defile, 42/34.
fyaunce, *sb.* trust, 86/89.
fychede, *vb.* 3 *pl. pt.* fixed, 70/242.
fyle, *vb. inf.* defile, 68/182; fylede, *pp.* 93/28.

G.

gapaunde, *vb. prp.* gaping, 70/246.
garnere, *sb.* granary, 58/1.
garrys, *vb.* 3 *sg. pr.* makes, 116/39.
gase, *vb.* 3 *sg. pr.* goes, 90/54.
gastely, *adj.* spiritual, 10/28.
gate, *vb.* 3 *sg. pt.* begot, 75/11.
gates, *sb. pl.* roads, ways, 101/144, 119/16.
gayne, *adj.* convenient, 101/144.
gayt, *vb.* 2 *pl. pr.* get, 115/8.
gedyre, *vb. inf.* gather, include, 35/9; gedire, *sg. imper.* 48/18; gedyrde, *pp.* 48/19; gedirde, 32/12.
gelery, *sb.* deceit, trickery, 13/20.
gelouse, *adj.* jealous, 58/22.
gente, *adj.* noble, 97/15.
gere, *vb.* 3 *sg. pr.* causes, 13/8; gerte, *pp.* 7/4.
germandir, *sb.* (?) some precious stone, 97/15.
gerne, *adv.* eagerly, 101/143.
gernere, *sb.* garner, 53/24.

geste, *sb.* guest, 91/91.
gete, *sb.* jet, 97/15.
getes, *vb.* 3 *pl. pr.* beget, 5/33; getyn, *pp.* 4/9; get, 98/29.
gome, *sb.* man, 98/29.
gouernaylle, *sb.* ruler, 35/10.
grauen, *vb. pp.* buried, 29/12.
graythely, *adj.* well-formed, excellent, worthy, 98/29.
graythely, *adv.* quickly, readily, 101/144.
grete, *vb. inf.* cry, 103/187; grett, 3 *pl. pt.* 103/187.
greuosere, *adj. cp.* more grievous, more harmful, 14/18.
grewe, *sb.* Greek, 47/8.
gruche, *vb.* 2 *sg. imp.* grudge, 49/36.
grysse, *sb.* grass, 22/5.
gulyardy, *sb.* buffoonery, ribaldry, 37/6.
gun, *vb.* 3 *sg. pt.* began, 71/276, 92/20; 2 *sg. pt.* 72/336.
gysed, *vb.* 2 *sg. pt.* didst prepare, 101/143.

H.

habyde, *vb. inf.* abide, wait for, 89/47; habade, 3 *sg. pt.* 19/22.
hailsed, *vb.* 3 *pl. pt.* hailed, 101/149.
haldande, *sb. pl.* holders, possessors, 31/8.
halden, *vb. pp.* bound (under obligation), 38/13.
hale, *adj.* whole, sound, 8/26.
hally, *adj.* holy, 1/20, 27.
haloghes, *sb.* saints, 77/17; halous, 21/7; halowes, 5/28.
hape, *sb.* (good) fortune, 115/13.
hase, *vb.* 3 *sg. pr.* has, 1/21, 3/27; 3 *pl. pr.* 1/20, 2/8, 7/25.
hateredyn, *sb.* hatred, 12/24, 25/21, 41/1.
hatten, *vb. pp.* called, 12/21.
haunkede, *vb. pp.* entangled, 12/10.
hauntede, *vb. pp.* practised, 14/5.
hauynge, *sb.* possessions, power, 6/9.
hawe, *sb.* haw (fruit of hawthorn), 90/63, 118/76.
heghe, *adj.* high, 3/11.
heghenees, *sb.* haughtiness, 12/15.
heghyng, *sb.* exaltation, 24/6.
heide, *sb.* head, 109/60.
heldes, *vb.* 3 *sg. pr.* inclines, 25/18; helde, 3 *sg. pt.* 44/21.
hele, *sb.* health, salvation, 3/25, 5/34, 9/6.
hele, *vb. inf.* conceal, 46/7; helede, 3 *sg. pt.* 46/12.

Glossary. 125

heledide, *vb.* 3 *pl. pt.* submitted, 104/230.
helelynge, *sb* concealing, 6/17.
helere, *sb.* healer, saviour, 67/140.
hende, *adj.* gracious, 99/80; hendeste, *super.* 104/229.
hendely, *adv.* graciously, 57/11.
herber(e), *vb. inf.* harbour, shelter, 9/28, 30/13.
herbery, *sb.* harbour, refuge, 30/19.
herere, *sb.* hearer, 12/30.
herne-panne, *sb.* skull, 69/226.
heryede, *vb.* 3 *sg. pt.* harried, 4/19.
hete, *vb.* 1 *sg. pr.* tell, promise, 89/50.
hete, *vb.* 1 *sg. pr.* grow hot, 112/150.
hethyng(e), *sb.* scorn, contempt, ridicule, 40/25, 42/33, 68/200.
heþen, *adv.* hence, 9/7, 105/261.
heuede, *sb.* head, power, 5/34; *adj.* chief, 12/2, 8.
heuenes, *sb.* heaviness, 14/2.
hey, *adj.* high, 4/30.
heyn, *adv.* hence, 85/70.
hide, *vb. pp.* hidden, 59/20.
highte, *vb.* 3 *sg. pt.* was called, 61/15, 16.
hippynge, *sb.* jumping over or omitting part of the service, 40/26.
homerynge, *sb.* muttering, 40/26.
horssyng, *sb.* equipage, 24/30.
howgates, *adv.* in what manner, how, 27/2.
hyen, *adv.* hence, 117/66.
hyghte, *vb.* 2 *sg. pt.* promised, 23/26; hyghttes, 3 *sg. pt.* 59/15.
hyne, *sb. pl.* servants, 104/230.
hynge, *vb. inf.* hang, 100/92.

I.

in-gate, *sb.* entrance, 53/9, 57/3.
inmanges, *prep.* among, 48/1.
inspayre, *sb.* breathing, breath, 75/7.
intill, *prep.* into, 10/33.
inwyttes, *sb. pl.* senses, 116/42.

iage, *sb.* jerk, 70/243.

K.

kan, *vb.* 2 *sg. pr.* knowest, 19/35.
kawl, *vb. inf.* call, 115/3.
kele, *vb. inf.* cool, 107/7; 3 *sg. pr.* 19/29.
kenn, *vb. inf.* teach, make known, 35/8; kennes, 3 *sg. pr.* 11/18, 16/20; kennde, 3 *sg. pt.* 31/30; kende, *pp.* 14/23, 22/31.

kennynge, *sb.* instruction, 22/24.
kide, *vb.* 2 *sg. pt.* didst show, 66/101.
knaue, *sb.* servant, 6/31, 102/168.
knaweliggynge, *sb.* knowledge, 59/19.
konn, *vb.* 3 *sg. pr.* knows, 29/36.
kychynnere, *sb.* cook, 56/20.
kye, *sb. pl.* cows, 22/20.
kynd(e), *sb.* nature, 3/28, 4/29, 32, 12/16.
kyndely, *adv.* by nature, 14/7, 8.
kynredyn, *sb.* kindred, 18/29.

L.

lache, *vb. inf.* seize, 13/32; laghte, 3 *sg. pt.* 105/258.
laddes, *sb. pl.* lads, men, 100/116.
lame, *sb.* loam, 88/5.
lange, *vb. inf.* long, 93/41.
langes, *vb.* 3 *pl. pr.* belongs, 1/27; langande, *prp.* 30/16.
large, *adj.* liberal, generous, 49/10, 13, 75/421.
latesommes, *sb.* tardiness, backwardness, 13/32.
lattly, *adv.* late, 18/13.
lawe, *adj.* low, 38/19.
lawede, *adj.* unlearned, lay, 5/26.
lawede, *vb.* 3 *sg. pt.* lowered, humbled, 34/7.
layke, *sb.* sport, amusement, 40/25.
laytheste, *adj.* most hateful, 100/115.
ledden, *vb.* 3 *pl. pt.* led, 100/116.
lede, *sb.* man, person, people, land, 97/20, 100/115, 103/211, 104/243.
lefe, *vb. inf.* leave, abandon, 35/30.
leffe, *vb.* 1 *sg. pr.* believe, trust, 74/410.
lefte, *vb.* 3 *sg. pr.* lift, 48/20.
lefulle, *adv.* permissible, lawful, 8/4.
lele, *adj.* faithful, 32/26.
lelly, *adv.* faithfully, 26/24, 95/87.
len, *vb. inf.* give, lend, 109/55; lennes, 2 *sg. pr.* 77/5.
lende, *vb. inf.* remain, reside, tarry, 98/47, 99/78, 103/211; 3 *sg. pr.* 80/47.
lere, *vb. inf.* teach, learn, 2/10, 30; leres, 3 *sg. pr.* 26/8; lere, 3 *pl. pr.* 2/27; lerede, *pp.* 2/5.
lerede, *adj.* learned, 5/26, 8/7.
leryng, *sb.* learning, 1/26.
les(s)e, *vb. inf.* loose, 6/22, 7/4.
lesses, *vb.* 3 *sg. pr.* lessens, 24/16.
lessynge, *sb.* lessening, 9/7.
lesynge, *sb.* lying, 92/4; *pl.* lies, 6/21.

126 Glossary.

lete by, vb. 3 sg. pt. esteem, value, 97/20; lett, 3 pl. pt. 103/192.
lettes, vb. 3 sg. pr. hinders, 11/30, 14/3, 78/3; lettis, 3 pl. pr. 26/4.
leue, sb. belief, 14/16.
leue, vb. 1 pl. pr. believe, 5/13.
leue, adj. dear, beloved, 54/19.
lewde, adj. unlearned, lay, 8/7.
lewte, sb. loyalty, 57/24.
lodde, sb. people, men, 90/55.
lofe, vb. inf. praise, glorify, 34/1; louede, pp. 33/9.
loos, sb. praise, 24/28.
lorne, vb. pp. lost, 67/141.
losengery, sb. flattery, 26/6.
lowssynge, sb. loosing, setting free, 9/16.
lowte, vb. 1 pl. pr. bow, worship, 5/13.
lufe-frayners, sb. pl. love-seekers, 62/7.
lugede, vb. pp. lodged, 97/5.
lurdans, sb. pl. lazy persons, rascals, 100/115.
lyfelade, sb. livelihood, 6/8.
lygge, vb. inf. lie, 59/28.
lyghte, adj. easy, 18/21.
lyghtenes, sb. alleviation, ease, 9/5, 40/33, 41/6.
lyghtly, adv. easily, 14/6.
lyghtnes, vb. 3 sg. pr. enlightens, 59/19.
lykande, adj. pleasing, 12/15.
lykede, vb. 3 sg. pt. pleased, 92/16.
lyknes, sb. comparison, 24/18.
lykynge, sb. pleasure, 5/29, 11/30.
lyne, sb. linen, 22/20.
lyte, sb. tardiness, 13/32.
lythe, sb. people, men, tenants, 6/26, 7/5; lythes, 98/48.

M.

male-eese, sb. distress, discomfort, 19/31.
malese, sb. malice, 61/18.
mane, sb. complaint, 80/29.
mase, vb. 3 sg. pr. makes, 17/10; 3 pl. pr. 58/25.
maun, vb. 1 pl. pr. must, 8/23.
mawmetis, sb. pl. idols, 103/216.
mawmetryes, sb. idolatries, 5/15.
mayne, sb. power, 91/87, 101/140.
maystry, sb. mastery, dominion, 103/216.
medles, adj. profitless, 40/26.
mekill, adj. & adv. much, many, 1/19, 20, 2/4.

mekillnes, sb. greatness, 80/32.
mekyde, vb. pp. humbled, made meek, 22/30.
mele, vb. inf. speak, 103/186.
mene, vb. inf. moan, communicate, tell, 98/28, 44; 1 sg. pr. 85/51.
menesyng, sb. mention, 98/34.
mengede, vb. pp. mixed, 5/3.
menskede, vb. 3 pl. pt. honoured, 105/255.
menʒe, sb. household, 24/30, 104/234.
merrede, vb. 3 sg. pt. hindered, 103/215.
merres, vb. 3 sg. pr. hinders, 88/4.
merryng, sb. marring, impairment, 4/6.
mesure, sb. moderation, 28/13.
mete, adj. fit, meet, 4/30.
methe, adj. modest, 99/57.
methe, or methefulness, sb. temperance, 11/28.
mett, sb. measure, 11/32.
mobles, sb. pl. movable goods, 98/43.
moghte, vb. 3 sg. pr. might, 18/1, 6.
momellynge, sb. mumbling, 40/26.
mon, vb. 3 sg. pr. will, 89/41; 1 pl. pr. 90/75; 2 pl. pr. 54/11.
mone, vb. sg. imp. communicate, tell, 104/239.
mortasse, sb. mortise, 70/242.
mot, vb. 3 sg. pr. must, 62/14.
mouande, vb. prp. moving, 64/43.
mukke, sb. muck, 17/21.
mune, vb. 1 sg. pr. shall, 116/30.
mute, vb. inf. plead, 118/73.
mynynge, sb. lessening, 4/6.
mysdose, vb. 3 pl. pr. do amiss, 10/4.
mysese, sb. distress, misery, 30/23.
myster, sb. need, 9/31, 25/35, 27/9, &c.
mystraste, vb. inf. doubt, 36/8.
mytir, sb. mitre, 105/255.

N.

namely, adv. especially, 2/13.
nate, sb. pl. cattle, 22/19.
neddyrs, sb. pl. adders, 17/24.
nede, adv. of necessity, 47/14, 21.
neese, sb. nose, 17/1; nese, 48/31.
neghe, vb. inf. approach, 110/86.
nesche, vb. inf. soften, 33/11.
neuen, vb. 1 pl. pr. name, 5/22; neuenede, pp. 13/4; nevynn, inf. 17/23.

noblaye, *sb.* splendour, grandeur, 12/16.
noresche, *vb. inf.* nourish, 64/44.
noyande, *adj.* hurtful, 22/22, 65/63.
noye, *vb. inf.* annoy, hurt, 22/29.
noye, *sb.* hurt, injury, 26/6, 88/6.
nyende, *adj.* ninth, 6/24.

O.

o, *prep.* of, from, 90/55.
oftesythe(s), *adv.* often, 2/6, 13/7.
okyr, *sb.* usury, 13/19.
one, *prep.* in, on, 2/16, 3/2, 4/21, &c.
or, *adv.* before, 90/54.
orloge, *sb.* timepiece, 60/16, 17.
ouerhope, *sb.* over-confidence, 11/2.
ouermekill, *adv.* too much, 11/24.
ouer-tane, *vb. pp.* overcome, 58/10.
ouþer ... or, *conj.* either ... or, -37/30.
owterage, *sb.* excess, 11/29.

P.

parischennes, *sb.* parishioners, 2/26.
pay(e), *sb.* satisfaction, 107/2, 117/50.
pay(e), *vb. inf.* please, satisfy, 10/27, 40/23, 57/20; payes, 3 *pl. pr.* 56/1.
pelars, *sb. pl.* pillars, 52/36.
penetancere, *sb.* one who imposes penance, confessor, 58/32.
perawnter, *adv.* peradventure, 2/8.
pereles, *adj.* peerless, 98/38.
perry, *sb.* precious stones, 97/16.
pertenande, *adj.* pertaining, 28/8.
petance, *sb.* share, provision, 59/13.
pete, *sb.* pity, 20/23.
poleschesy, *sb.* 57/30.
pouste, *sb.* power, 68/168, 98/38.
preste, *adv.* quickly, readily, 91/91.
preue, *adj.* intimate, 99/83.
pungede, *vb. pp.* pricked, 109/60.
pure, *adj.* poor, 11/14, 31/3, 117/45.
puruaye, *vb. inf.* provide, 28/22; purvayede, *pp.* provided, 22/15.
purueance, *sb.* providence, 76/19.
pyssmowre, *sb.* ant, 22/33.
pystill, *sb.* epistle, 2/12, 11/8.

Q.

qwaynte, *adj.* skilful, clever, 18/1.
qwayntyse, *sb.* skill, wisdom, 108/38.
qweire, *sb.* choir, 40/14.
qwerte, *sb.* sound health, 108/30.
qwykke, *adj.* living, 3/29, 65/74.
qwylles, *adv.* while, 115/6.

R.

racede, *vb.* 3 *sg. pt.* tore, 69/219.
rathely, *adv.* quickly, 90/64.
raue, *vb.* 3 *pl. pt.* broke, opened, 44/24, 70/245.
rauesches, *vb.* 3 *sg. pr.* ravishes, 56/15; raueschede, *pp.* 58/10.
raughte, *vb. pp.* reached, given, 89/49.
rawe, *sb.* row, 89/37.
reall, *adj.* royal; 67/142.
relyede, *vb.* 3 *sg. pt.* rallied, 97/6.
resafe, *vb. inf.* receive, 57/11; reschayfe, 27/1; rescheyue, 8/28; ressayfes, 2 *sg. pr.* 45/28; ressayues, 3 *pl. pr.* 7/28; ressayfede, 2 *sg. pt.* 45/28; rescheyuede, *pp.* 17/29.
reste, *sb.* arrest, 25/12.
reuer, *sb.* river, 52/5.
reuthe, *sb.* sorrow, sadness, 94/61.
reuyng, *sb.* robbing, 6/16.
rewly, *adv.* sadly, dreadfully, 89/37.
rewme, *sb.* realm, 55/14.
ruggede, *vb.* 3 *sg. pt.* tore, 90/66.
rynnand, *adj.* smooth, fluent, 36/31.
rysesynge, *sb.* rising, 4/26.
ryste, *sb.* rest, peace, 53/6, 55/16, &c.
ryuely, *adv.* frequently, 7/9.

S.

saghe, *vb.* 1 *pl. pt.* saw, 35/23; 2 *sg. pt.* 84/40.
salfe, *vb. imp.* salve, 109/68.
samen, *adv.* together, 3/33, 9/15, 10/32; samenly, 3/14.
sane, *vb. inf.* heal, 93/40. *Cotgr.* 'Saner. To cure, heal, or make whole.'
sassyng, *sb.* holding, observing, 67/157.
sauoyre, *sb.* pleasure, 59/8, 19.
saynede, *vb.* 2 *sg. pt.* didst bless, 102/173, 104/227, 228.
schede, *vb. inf.* divide, separate, 64/45.
schenchipe, *sb.* ignominy, punishment, 22/16.
schente, *vb. pp.* disgraced, confounded, 84/34.
schere, *vb. inf.* cut, 67/161.
schire, *adj.* pure, 59/11.
scho, *pron.* she, 35/2, 4.
schope, *vb.* 3 *sg. pt.* shaped, created, 75/3.

Glossary.

schoris, *sb. pl.* pangs, pains, 116/39.
schotte, *vb.* 3 *sg. pr.* 120/34.
sckathe, *vb. inf.* injure, 27/33.
segge, *sb.* man, 101/142.
seghes, *vb.* 3 *sg. pr.* sees, 46/26.
sek(e)nes, *sb.* sickness, 4/24, 9/5, 30.
sekerly, *adv.* securely, certainly, 38/13.
sekyr, *adj.* secure, 10/28.
selcouthe, *adj.* strange, wonderful, 100/88.
sely, *adj.* happy, 54/5; cely, 54/17.
sembyll, *vb. inf.* assemble, gather, 57/31.
semle, *sb.* meeting, battle, 101/142.
sen, *conj.* since, 43/26, 46/28.
sere, *adj.* several, particular, 3/18, 12/18, 65/62, 98/36; *adv.* severally, 65/59.
serues, *vb.* 3 *sq. pr.* deserves, 5/2.
sesede, *vb. pp.* seized, possessed, 72/340.
seyn, *adv.* afterwards, 93/27.
seynge, *sb.* seeing, 16/24.
seys, *vb.* 3 *sg. pr.* sees, 58/11.
skikk ande skekke, *vb. inf.* rob and plunder, 90/59.
skillwyse, *adj.* possessed of reason, reasonable, 1/14, 8/31, 9/4.
skornande, *vb. pp.* mocking, 69/228.
skourgegynge, *sb.* scourging, 69/215.
skowreghide, *vb. pp.* scourged, 69/211.
skyll, *sb.* reason, 1/8, 22/19.
skyum, *sb.* scum, 18/26.
sla(a), *vb. inf.* slay, 27/14, 85/65; 1 *pl. pr.* 6/5; 3 *pl. pr.* 12/9; slaas, 3 *sg. pr.* 12/13; slaes, 27/17; slane, *pp.* 80/31.
slake, *vb. inf.* slacken, 95/105.
slawenes, *sb.* sloth, 13/29.
sleghenes, *sb.* wisdom, sagacity, 11/17.
sleghte, *sb.* wisdom, sagacity, 11/16.
slewthe, *sb.* sloth, 13/29.
slokyns, *vb.* 3 *sg. pr.* extinguishes, 25/8.
slyke, *adj.* such, 56/32, 58/13.
smate, *vb.* 3 *sg. pt.* smote, 43/1.
sonne, *adv.* soon, 35/29.
sothefaste, *adj.* true, 3/11, 8/18; sothefastly, *adv.* 8/13.
sowe, *vb. inf.* grieve, 85/72.
sown, *vb. inf.* sound, 12/24.
sownnes, *vb.* 3 *sg. pr.* sounds, 48/7.
sparre, *vb.* 2 *sg. imp.* bar, close, 53/7.
spensere, *sb.* butler, steward, 56/33.

speres, *vb.* 3 *sg. pr.* bars, fastens, 57/2.
spire, *vb. inf.* inquire, 88/2.
spousebreke, *sb.* adultery, 14/18.
spyll, *vb. inf.* destroy, perish, 72/324, 93/39.
spytt, *for* spyll, *vb. inf.* 114/18.
stabill, *vb. inf.* establish, 55/14; stabylls, 3 *sg. pr.* 58/6.
stalleworthe, *adj.* stalwart, strong, 8/14.
stalworthenes, *sb.* strength, stalwartness, 25/33, 26/11.
stallworthy, *adv.* stalwartly, courageously, 26/9.
stamerynge, *sb.* hesitation, 14/10.
stedde, *vb. inf.* place, 109/75.
stede, *sb.* place, 8/17, 22/14.
steighe, *vb.* 3 *sg. pt.* ascended, 29/15; stey(e), 4/28, 33; stey, 2 *sg. pt.* 73/367.
steke, *vb.* 2. *sg. imp.* shut, close, 53/11.
steskys *for* stekys, *vb.* 3 *sg. pr.* fastens, shuts, 53/4.
steuene, *sb.* voice, 79/11.
stowrrys, *sb. pl.* conflicts, pangs, 106/12.
strange, *adj.* strong, 55/6.
strayke, *vb.* 3 *pl. pr.* rub gently, 120/33.
strydand, *prp.* striving, throbbing (with more than usual force), 70/248.
strynde, *sb.* generation, 93/27.
stynte, *vb. inf.* stop, 72/339.
styre, *vb. inf.* move, 67/162.
sudayne, *adj.* sudden, 76/36, 77/20.
suellynge, *sb.* swallowing, 17/1; sweloynge, *sb.* 48/25.
suget, *sb.* subject, 64/41; sugettes, *pl.* church-members, parishioners, 2/27, 31.
suggeourned, *vb.* 2 *sg. pt.* didst sojourn, 101/141.
surquytry, *sb.* presumption, 24/10.
suyle, *sb.* soil, country, 101/141.
swelowe, *vb. inf.* swallow, 70/254; swelawes, 3 *sg. pr.* 48/31.
swetis, *vb.* 3 *sg. pr.* sweats, 56/22.
sybb(e), *adj.* near of kin, related, 6/11, 14/20, 99/69.
syll, *sb.* floor, earth, 103/201.
syment, *sb.* cement, 52/31.
synner, *sb.* (?) error in transcription, 114/18.
synows, *sb. pl.* sinews, 69/236.
syte, *sb.* pain, 12/21.
sythes, *sb. pl.* times, 18/4.

Glossary.

T.

taa, *vb.* 2 *sg. pr.* take, 111/112; tase, 3 *sg. pr.* 8/32, 33; 3 *pl. pr.* 9/9; tane, *pp.* 4/17, 7/34, &c.
tades, *sb. pl.* toads, 17, 24.
taken, *vb. pp.* indicated, 38/14.
tane, *adj.* one, 7/11.
temperoure, *sb.* temper, 25/3.
tente, *vb. inf.* try, 5/29.
thede, *sb.* people, country, 100/113.
thee-banes, *sb. pl.* thigh-bones, 45/2.
thewe, *sb.* virtue, 10/19, 27; *pl.* 52/16, 57/9.
thir, *pron. nom. pl.* these, 4/1.
thole, *vb. inf.* suffer, 70/271; tholede, 2 *sg. pt.* 70/272; 3 *sg. pt.* 4/12, 56/18.
thole-mode, *adj.* patient, 10/3.
thonour, *sb.* thunder, 114/4.
thraly, *adv.* boldly, severely, 100/114.
threhed, *sb.* trinity, 63/7.
threted, *vb.* 3 *pl. pt.* oppressed, 100/114.
thweyn, *vb. inf.* (?) (a word ending in *-in* is wanted, to rhyme with *sin*).
till, *prep.* to, 1/27, 4/2, 9/34, &c.
tite, *adv.* soon, quickly, 20/1.
to-braste, *vb.* 3 *pl. pt.* burst asunder, 69/236.
to-reuen, *vb. pp.* torn, 69/213.
tother, toþer, *adj.* other, second, 3/11, 7/12, 11/7.
traiste, *vb. inf.* trust, hope, 10/33, 11/2; traystes, 3 *pl. pr.* 5/17.
trauelde, *vb. pp.* troubled, 18/15.
tray, *sb.* trouble, annoyance, 1/25.
trayste, *sb.* trust, faith, 10/30, 31, 28/17.
traystely, *adv.* trustfully, confidently, 36/15.
trouthe, *sb.* faith, belief, 45/23, 46/10.
trow(e), *vb. inf.* believe, 3/9, 10, 47/4; trowes, 1 *pl. pr.* 45/24; trowande, *prp.* 21/5.
trowyng, *sb.* believing, 38/17.
twesste, *adj.* twelfth, 67/163.
twyn, *adj.* two, 13/17.
twyn, *vb. inf.* separate, 18/3, 21/12; twynnede, *pp.* 33/16.
tyne, *vb. inf.* lose, 111/124; tynes, 2 *sg. pr.* 40/20; tynt(e), *pp.* 17/31, 19/17, 66/128.
tyte, *adv.* soon, quickly, 23/26, 32/27.
tythandes, *sb. pl.* tidings, 112/142.

Þ.

þan, *pron. acc.* them, 18/33.
þase, *pron.* those, 12/1.
þere, *adj.* these, 38/20.
þof(e), *conj.* though, 7/6, 33/29, 40/8.
þusgate, *adv.* in this way, thus, 20/11.

V.

venqwyste, *vb. pp.* vanquished, 94/75.
verray, *adj.* true, 45/26, 79/5, 86/87.
verraymente, *adv.* truly, 84/36.
versy, *vb. imp.* repeat verses, 40/16.
vesete, *vb. inf.* visit, 9/29.
vesettis, *vb.* 3 *sg. pr.* clothes, 90/73; vesete, *pp.* 20/20.
vgglynes, *sb.* abhorrence, detestation, 45/18.
vmbethynke, *vb. sg. imp.* think, take heed, 17/27, 26/34.
vmbythynkynge, *sb.* meditation, 17/16.
vmbylowkede, *vb. pp.* included, 7/10.
vn-bouxsomnes, *sb.* disobedience, 12/19, 24/7.
vndirlowttes, *sb.* dependants, 2/13.
vndirtane, *vb. pp.* undertaken, 55/10.
vndreghe, *adj.* impatient, 113/171.
vndrone, *sb.* the time about 9 o'clock in the morning, 43/7, 73/376.
vnhamlynes, *sb.* want of familiarity, affectation, 12/19.
vnkyndly, *adj.* unnatural, 24/6.
vnmyste, *adj.* (?) not missed, obtained, 105/255.
vnskilwyse, *adj.* unreasonable, 13/5.
vnthewes, *sb. pl.* vices, 57/1.
vntill, *prep.* unto, 2/22, 9/22, 10/7.
vppe-rysynge, *sb.* resurrection, 3/26.

W.

wakire, *adj.* watchful, 54/20, 60/15.
wakkyn, *vb. inf.* wake up, 60/16; wakyns, 3 *pl. pr.* 60/18, 19; wakenede, *pp.* 60/26.
wandes, *sb. pl.* rods, 102/171.
wandreth, *sb.* misery, distress, 11/23.
wanes, *sb. pl.* dwellings, houses, property, 98/45.
waresche, *vb.* 3 *sg. pr.* protects, cures, 25/30.
warre, *adj.* cautious, 54/20.
was, *sb.* torch, 91/89.

wate, *vb.* 1 *sg. pr.* know, 34/10; 2 *sg. pr.* 30/32; 3 *sg. pr.* 9/3.
wathes, *sb. pl.* dangers, 11/17.
wattyr, *sb.* water, 114/15.
wawkes, *sb.* watch, dying person, 115/1.
waxande, *vb. prp.* growing, 21/32.
wayke, *adj.* weak, 55/9.
wayknes, *sb.* weakness, 41/2.
wele, *adv.* well, 3/33.
weled, *vb.* 3 *pl. pt.* chose, 105/252.
wemles, *adj.* without harm or blemish, spotless, 20/21, 67/133.
wende, *vb. inf.* go, 3/33.
wenys, *vb.* 3 *sg. pr.* thinks, 24/11.
were, *sb.* doubt, 8/8.
werede, *vb.* 2 *sg. pt.* didst keep off, 99/56.
weryede, *vb.* 3 *pl. pt.* cursed, 103/195.
wetandly, *adv.* knowingly, 7/3, 72/314.
whanhope, *sb.* despair, 10/33.
whatekyn, *adj.* what kind of, 89/35.
wheþer so, *pron.* whoever, whichever, 5/2, 14/21.
wheþer-som, *adv.* wheresoever, 41/33.
whethir, *conj.* still, nevertheless, 8/16.
whethire so, *pron.* whichsoever, 11/23.
wiet(e), *vb. inf.* know, 9/23, 26/19; 2 *sg. imp.* 21/21.
wighte, *adj.* strong, vigorous, 57/26.
wilnes, *vb.* 3 *sg. pr.* desires, 12/33.
with, *prep.* by, 4/13.
witte, *sb.* knowledge, 23/34.
witterly, *adv.* surely, 60/29.
witterwyssynge, *sb.* guidance, instruction, 14/10.
witty, *adj.* wise, 55/21.
woddyse, *sb. pl.* woods, 114/14.
wode, *adj.* mad, 71/305.
wodnese, *sb.* madness, 114/15.

wone, *sb.* store, plenty, 102/179; wane, 102/181.
wonn, *vb. inf.* live, dwell, 82/80; wonne, 1 *sg. pr.* 76/44.
wonnynge, *sb.* dwelling, 64/40.
worthe, *vb. inf.* become, 61/25.
wounte, *vb.* 3 *sg. pt.* was accustomed, 48/1; *pp.* 13/20.
wreke, *vb. inf.* avenge, 12/33.
wrenkis, *sb. pl.* wiles, tricks, 55/5.
wrethe, *sb.* anger, wrath, 12/31, 107/10.
wrethe, *vb. inf.* anger, 71/292; 2 *sg. imp.* 50/1.
wyes, *sb. pl.* men, 102/159.
wyet(e), *vb. inf.* know, 17/26, 21/23.
wyghtes, *sb. pl.* creatures, 61/35.
wyll, *adj.* wild, ignorant, self-willed, 9/35.
wyllosay, *sb.* (what) wilt-thou-say, or, more probably an exclamation like *walaway*, 117/52.
wyllylyere, *adv.* more readily, 60/17.
wysse, *vb. inf.* guide, teach, show, 9/35, 72/319; *sg. imp.* 97/13; wysses, 3 *sg. pr.* 11/17.
wytes, *vb.* 3 *sg. pr.* departs, goes, 107/4.

3.

ȝelde, *vb. inf.* requite, 95/86.
ȝeme, *vb. inf.* take care of, keep, observe, 79/19; ȝemes, 3 *sg. pr.* 7/19, 11/30, 53/33.
ȝerely, *adv.* year by year, 58/24.
ȝerne, *vb. inf.* desire, 6/32; 1 *pl. pr.* 6/24, 29; ȝernes, 3 *sg. pr.* 5/30.
ȝode, *vb.* 3 *sg. pt.* went, 41/33, 99/71.
ȝolden, *vb. pp.* paid, 26/25.
ȝonge, *adj.* young, 102/183.

Y.

ynence, *prep.* anent, concerning, against, 26/30, 34/13.
yrke, *vb. inf.* to feel dislike, 25/7.

INDEX OF NAMES.

A.
Apocalips, 101/130.
Asye, Asia, 100/101.
Atemperance, Waiter, 56/27.
Austyn, Saynt, 22/13, 36/2, 59/26.

B.
Barthilmewe, Saynte, 55/28, 32.
Bedleme, 97/7.
Bernarde, Sayne, 16/20, 31/2, 59/31.
Bowsomnes, Damsel, 52/17.

C.
Charite, Abbess, 54/4.
Contemplacione, Builder, 53/14.
Craton, 103/210.
Curtasye, Receiver of Guests, 57/10.

D.
Damesele Conande and Wysse, þat es callede Meditacyone, Storekeeper, 57/29.
Danyele, 55/12.
Dauid, 52/29.
Denyse, Saynte, 58/20.
Deuocion, Cellaress, 53/23, 56/16.
Discrecyone, Treasurer, 55/21.
Domycyane, Domitian, 100/111, 101/141.
Drede, Porteress, 56/35.
Drucyane, 102/153.

E.
Envye, Damsel, 61/15.
Ephesym, Ephesus, 101/144.

F.
False Demynge of Oþer, Damsel, 61/17.
Forte, Damsel, 52/35.

G.
Gabrielle, 39/3.
Gaytryge, Dan Iohn, 1/1.
Gelosye, Time-keeper, 60/14.
Gregore, Saynt, 37/7.
Gruchynge, Damsel, 61/16.

H.
Herod, 69/206.
Honeste, Mistress of the Novices, 57/5.

I.
Iewes, 68/194, 196, 69/231.
Iewry, 70/259.
Ihesu Criste, 31/1, &c.
Iob, 59/31.
Iohn, Sayn, 11/7, 14/34, 68/174.
Iourdane, 68/175.
Iubilacion, Chantress, 56/5.
Iudas, 68/193, 71/298, 304.

K.
Katerin, Saynt, 119/10.

L.
Largesse, Nurse, 57/28.
Lewte, Nurse, 57/24.
Longyous, Longinus, 119/2.
Luffe of Clennes, Maiden, 51/14.

M.
Margarete, Saynt, 119/9.
Marye, Saynte, 79/1, 84/35.
Mathewe, Sayne, 9/24.
Meditacion, Builder, 53/24.
Meditacyone, Store-keeper, 57/30.
Mekenes, Maiden, 51/19.
Meknes, Sub-prioress, 54/29.
Mercy, Almoner, 56/34.
Michaelle, 39/3.
Miserecorde, Damsel, 52/18.

N.
Nabogodhonosore, 55/13.
Nassyngton, William, 63.

O.
Olyuere, Cragge of, 120/31.
Oracion, Builder, 53/14.
Orysone, Chantress, 55/23.

P.
Pathmos, Patmos, 101/129.
Paule, Sayn, 2/12, 16/5, 40/11.

Index of Names.

Penance, Cook, 56/20.
Pete, Butler or Pittancer, 56/32, 58/32.
Pilate, 69/210, 212, 232.
Poleschesy, Store-keeper, 57/30.
Porte Latyn, 100/116.
Pouerte, Maiden, 51/20.
Predicacion, Builder, 53/13.
Pride, Damsel, 61/16.

R.

Raphaelle, 39/3.
Resone, Purveyor, 57/22.

Rewfulnes, Builder, 53/23.
Rightwynes, Maiden, 51/14.
Rome, 55/13.

S.

Salomon, 52/25.
Scrifte, Builder, 53/13.
Sobirnes, Reader, 56/29.
Sufferance, Damsel, 52/35.
Symplese, Receiver of Guests, 57/15

W.

Wysdome, Prioress, 54/22.

The manufacturer's authorised representative in the EU for product safety is Oxford University Press España S.A. of el Parque Empresarial San Fernando de Henares, Avenida de Castilla, 2 – 28830 Madrid (www.oup.es/en or product.safety@oup.com). OUP España S.A. also acts as importer into Spain of products made by the manufacturer.

www.ingramcontent.com/pod-product-compliance
Ingram Content Group UK Ltd.
Pitfield, Milton Keynes, MK11 3LW, UK
UKHW022132220326
469240UK00006B/15